"SMILIN' SID" HATFIELD
Founding Father of American Overtime
A true story

Richard Beckett

Another Chapter Publishing

Copyright © 2021 by **Harry R. Beckett II**

All rights reserved. No part of this publication may be reproduced, distributed or transmitted in any form or by any means, without prior written permission of the author or publisher.

All images used in this title fall under the fair use act or were taken directly by the author.

Harry R. Beckett II/Another Chapter Publishing

Publisher's Note: Harry R. Beckett and Another Chapter Publishing assume no responsibility or liability for any errors or omissions in the content of this work. The information contained herein is provided on an "as is" basis with no guarantees of completeness, accuracy, usefulness or timeliness. Every effort has been made to provide factual information, while constructing the details into a story.

Book Layout © 2014 BookDesignTemplates.com

Smilin Sid Hatfield/ Harry R. Beckett II -- 1st ed.
Artistic Spaces Publishing is an imprint of Another Chapter Publishing
ISBN 978-0-9796328-6-0

HIS054000 History/Social History

Dedication

This book is dedicated to the hard working people of Mingo and Logan Counties in West Virginia. I believe the basic working rights all Americans enjoy today are derivatives of their struggle for fairness and fair pay.

CONTENTS

PART 1: CROSS THE RIVER 5
- THE BRIDGE 5
- THE WAY IT WAS 7
- THRESHOLD OF MODERN 9
- THE ROOT CAUSE 11
- SAFETY FIRST 13
- THE ADVERSARIES EVOLVE 17
- WHO WAS SID 21
- BLOODLINES 31
- LET'S CONTINUE WITH WILLIAM 35
- POWER EXPANDS 37
- A BIT ABOUT THOMAS 41
- IT STARTED WITH A KISS 43
- FLOYD GETS HIS 49

PART 2: REDNECKS, GUNS, AND LAWYERS 57
- ABOUT THAT EIGHT YEARS 57
- MATEWAN SIMMERS 59
- MILES TO GO 69
- THE IMPETUS FOR BLAIR MOUNTAIN 75
- THOMAS ZEROES IN 79
- THE ROAD TO WELCH 83
- THE MURDER OF SID 87
- BLAIR MOUNTAIN 91
- CLOUDS GATHER 95
- IN THE MEANTIME 99
- THE ORIGINAL REDNECK 101
- THE SHOOTING BEGINS 107

THE LAWYERS	111
THE SABER IS IN THE SABBARD	117
PART 3: THE BITTERSWEET YEARS	119
LAST GASPS OF A DYNESTY	119
PATIENCE, DEAR MINER	123
THE FINAL STRETCH TO OVERTIME	127
FINALLY, OVERTIME	131
HARRY'S VETO OVERTURNED	135
WHAT IT MEANS TODAY	141
PRACTICAL APPLICATION	143
REMEMBERING WIRT	149

PREFACE

I would like to tell a story. It's a story that a lot of people have already heard, so it's not exactly new. The story is about the labor disputes in the United States between the late 19th and early 20th centuries. This story is focused around the Appalachian coal mines. The conflicts that arose happened because there were no federal, state, or local laws controlling the number of hours an employee could work in a single day. Formal records of time worked were not required in this era. Children as young as 10 were allowed to earn a wage in the Appalachian mines, the New England sweatshops, the docks, the steel mills, and other industries of bustling America. That's just how it was at the time. It was the Lochner Era, an evolving and uncertain time before The Fair Labor Standards Act became law in 1938.

This was true everywhere in America, but it was especially true in the mountains of Appalachia. Most all-American industries exploited their workers. The workers in the coal mines of Appalachia faced the same oppression, but the difference was that their job was significantly more dangerous. It was literally life and death to work in a methane-filled cave with minimal safety oversight. It was bad for most all workers in America, but it was deadly for the Appalachian coal miners of 1920.

Whether you were born Irish, African American, Italian, Polish, or wherever, you were forced to unite against a totalitarian monarchy. You were forced to be inclusive. We Americans say we're a "Melting Pot" as a nation. The people in this story could not be a more perfect example of that melting pot.

For the most part, this story takes place in the coal fields of Southern West Virginia. The battles, the casualties and the tactics of this brutal journey are real. The United Mine Workers of America sought to protect and represent these miners. The union's ultimate goals were recognition, representation, safety, and a fair wage for all. The mining company's goal was to blast any attempt of organization. It's a fascinating and classic story about labor and management gone terribly wrong. It resulted in a real war, but it was an unknown war. The focus is mostly on the United Mine Workers of America and their bitter struggle to organize the miners in Southern West Virginia. Hopefully, I can relate a time that is nothing like anyone would experience today. These times were extreme, difficult, unfair, and dangerous. It was pretty dismal, in Mingo County, WV about 100 years ago.

By 1920, just about all the trade industries were represented by a recognized union, or were soon to be. The exception was the geography around one of the greatest seams of coal the world has ever known. That would be in Mingo and Logan counties in Southern West Virginia. It's part of the Pocahontas Coal Seam, and it's still producing coal today. This is a story about the oppressed people who came from all over the world, and how they came together because they had no other choice. It's a tribute to their sacrifices and endurance and to the family members they lost.

This is a true story. It's a story about the dangerous working conditions coal miners faced and what they went through just to survive. It happened in a town with no serious representative. That community was a collection of citizens and immigrants who were forced to comply with an employer who thought little of its workers. This void went on for years. Hope was just a casual word.

In large part, it's a story about then versus now. The oppressive culture the West Virginia miners faced during this era was awful. But they survived, even though many hundreds of them died in mine disasters. Some died from machine-gun fire. Some died from the Spanish Flu. But the vast majority of this culture survived. They were instrumental in delivering the working rights all Americans enjoy today.

It's a story about a skinny young man who walked over the Tug Fork footbridge to Matewan, and made things start to change. The winds of justice began to fill the sails of fate. It was time to hoist the encrusted anchor that laid on the seabed for far too long. Stuff was about to happen. This young man chose to make things better for these poor minors. In doing so, he also chose to make history.

That single guy was a rough and tumble kid from Blackberry, KY. He decided to be the first one who would actually do something to help the miners. It's also about the town he adopted. It's about what he did and what happened to him. It's about his legacy that helped change the labor laws of 1920 America. It's a classic story about the power of the minority controlling the majority—mostly against their will. Ultimately, I hope it gives everyone faith that Americans will always seek justice, truth, and fair play. It all begins in the small town of Matewan, West Virginia.

1920 Matewan, WV, Photo public domain

Photo hangs at the Hatfield McCoy Inn in Williamson, WV, which is a super cool place owned by super nice people. Sid Hatfield rented an apartment in the center building. It's called the Nenni Bldg. and you can still visit this place today.

Tug Fork River at Matewan.
This photo was taken at sunset in early June.

PART 1: CROSS THE RIVER

ꕥ The Bridge ꕥ

In Southern West Virginia, in the early 20th century, the coal miners' struggle against the brutal practices of the mining companies, their proxies, and to a lesser extent, the railroads, was mostly unknown to our nation. The characters and the events in this work are real. I traveled and worked in every town and hamlet in the locations I reference. I was a spice salesman for over 10 years in this region. It was my first job in the corporate world, and I was required to travel all of the highways and byways of this geography. It's a story that should rival the Hatfield & McCoy feud, but it doesn't. This story started just a few years after that iconic era ended, but it happened in the exact same place. My grandfathers and great-grandfathers could probably tell it better than me, but they are long since gone. So, I want to tell this story in honor of the brave people of Mingo County and Logan County, WV. This is where my family came from.

Matewan, West Virginia . . . 1919. That was the most likely year Sid Hatfield moved from Blackberry, KY to Matewan, WV, but I can't prove that. If true, the trip was short. All he had to do was cross the Tug Fork River. This is not a big river, at least not at Matewan. However, this was a big deal for American history. Considering the change that was about to happen, Sid's move may be as big as a double agent crossing the Glienicke Bridge in East Berlin a couple of generations later. I'm pretty sure he walked over the old footbridge connecting KY to WV. Most people did. The bridge pictured is long since gone.

Sid would change just about everything the townsfolk had known for a very long time. He would give them hope. He gave them a reason to reject the oppressive living and working conditions that almost everyone in this community experienced. He sparked the largest and greatest civil insurrection in American history—excluding the Civil War. Ultimately, he helped change the whole dynamic

Wooden suspension footbridge connecting Matewan, WV to Blackberry, KY. This bridge was used by Sid Hatfield, and everyone else. It was not designed for automobiles. The children pictured are unknown. The building on the far left is the fabled Blue Goose saloon on the KY side. It too is long since gone.

of labor practices, and labor laws, in Mingo County and throughout America. However, he would pay the ultimate price for doing so. Sid Hatfield finally said no. For more than 30 years, no one had the guts to utter that word to the mining company and their allies. That was something a rational person simply would not do. He got a lot of attention from the investors and the masterminds who wore top hats and smoked cigars in tall buildings that were far away from Mingo.

The Way it Was

The American workforce today is diverse and ever-changing. The notion that Americans work a 40-hour week, Monday through Friday, is pretty well challenged these days. Yet, this is still considered normal and customary. About every beer commercial you hear or see is centered around a weekend event. Certainly today, many people work on weekends, overnight, and commonly from their own homes. I have worked overnight for many assignments, so I get it. My wife works from home and she works long hours. Consider our firemen, our first responders, our air traffic controllers, our military, and those who work in the energy sector. Someone is always awake and monitoring the controls 24 hours a day. Still, everyone is governed by a set of labor laws that mandate overtime pay if our work exceeds 40 hours in a week. Children under the age of 16 are severely restricted by the number of hours they can work per week, and when they can work them. Minors between 16 and 18 have more work flexibility, but there are still many restrictions when compared to an adult.

In 1920 Matewan, this concept was unthinkable to the miners. The same went for the shopkeepers, the railmen, the blacksmiths, and just about every other occupation you could name. Many miners worked sunup to sundown, just so they could maintain a life of squalor and poverty. For many, their rent payment went to the company they worked for and was (often) more than half their income. If you had children, there wasn't much left to survive on, let alone save.

Such was also the understanding of the wives, the children, and neighbors of everyone except the wealthy investors who funded the railroads and the mining companies. What happened in early 20th century Mingo Co., versus what we understand today would shock just about anyone. Basically, the miners of Matewan, and in many other parts of Appalachia, were slaves to the coal mining companies, their proxies, and the railroad companies that transported the coal. The common people were suppressed by "detectives," who were paid by these companies to maintain the unfettered flow of coal to the industrial machine that was feeding a growing, international demand. The detectives were also instructed to prevent the miners from forming a union. A great struggle flourished between the desperate miners and the industrial giants that commanded them. The average worker knew something was wrong. The workers had no surrogate for justice. There was no one to help. And then suddenly, out of nowhere, a skinny, 5' 4" tall blacksmith from Blackberry, KY started telling the families and townsfolk of Matewan that something would be done. He understood the problem and he was going to change things.

Threshold of Modern

During the early time frame of this story, WWI had just ended, and affordable power was in high demand. Electricity was sweeping the nation, and it needed cheap fuel to feed its appetite. It needed coal, and few places had more affordable coal than Mingo and Logan counties in West Virginia. The roaring 20's was just getting started. Vast wealth was being created and new inventions were being spit out like popcorn at a theater. Many new inventions were powered by electricity. For example, Ernst Alexanderson created a high frequency alternator that powered the first successful radio transmission in 1920. William Potts, a Detroit police officer, created the first traffic light in 1920. The first portable hair dryer was also created in 1920. All of these new luxuries needed electricity to work, which needed coal to create the necessary power.

Among the waves of European immigrants pouring into America in the post war era, many were duped into believing a guaranteed job and affordable housing was just a train ride away. Imagine arriving at Ellis Island with nothing more than a carpet bag full of your stuff. In many cases, you would have your wife and kids with you. After several stormy weeks at sea, on a boat that really didn't want you, and then a harrowing inspection of your health and legal status at Ellis Island, you entered into New York City. Between 80 and 90 percent were allowed to pass. Upon arrival in the Big Apple, imagine seeing a well-dressed gentleman holding a sign advertising immediate employment, with guaranteed housing.

What would you do if you had no surrogate waiting to guide you in this strange new land? The mining companies knew these poor souls were easy prey to accept employment. And the chance of relatives following the immigrant's lead was very lucrative. They even paid recruiters to go to Europe and solicit immigrates to fulfil their hiring quotas. Many ended up in Southern West Virginia. Most had no concept they would become slaves to the endless supply of coal and the masters who controlled them. Most could not have known this would be the last time they would depart a train, or boat, or any other mode of transportation. Once they arrived in the coal town, it was almost like the 1976 hit song Hotel California by the legendary band The Eagles. "You can check out anytime you like, but you can never leave."

The Root Cause

There were relatively few federal labor laws in 1920 to prevent the mining and railroad companies from near total dominance over the people in much of Appalachia. If you lived in Matewan, and you worked for the mining company, it was common to live in housing owned by the same company you worked for. Not everyone experienced this, but many did. Therefore, you would pay your rent to the company who employed you. Many of these houses were nothing more than shelters. They were hastily built for the cheapest price. Demand for labor was skyrocketing, and the need to provide housing for these mostly immigrant laborers, and African-Americans from the deep South, was considered just another expense to the mining companies. This newfound gold mine needed labor, cheap labor, and the people who mined it had to live somewhere. The living conditions for many were like being detained at the Mexican border today, on their side.

Payday was typically on a Friday. To make matters worse, (in many but not all cases), the miner's paycheck was provided in the form of "script" currency. This form of money was printed, and coined, by the mining companies. It was manipulated in value, as well. In many cases, a miner could only cash his check at the general store in the village where he lived. Often, the stores were either owned by the mining company or heavily controlled by them. The miners and their family lived in an economic box canyon. There were scarce laws to protect them and even fewer elected sheriffs to maintain the laws that were actually enforceable. Miners lived at the mercy of their employer and their hired detectives. Imagine your paycheck being worth what your employer decided. It wasn't even U.S. currency. The company you worked for printed your paycheck. It's like going to a carnival and buying tickets to enjoy a particular attraction. The carnival sets the prices, and you decide if it's worth spending your money. You have to choose to pay for those tokens, tickets, or wrist bands to enter the park. You do so knowing you could leave anytime you wish. In Matewan, you didn't have that luxury. Neither did you have the option of buying many things you wanted, at a price you desired. It was take it or leave it. If you want more, either work harder, or join us.

Safety First

Imagine your employer warning you that if you join a union, or even tried to join a union, you would be evicted from your company-owned home. Imagine a band of heavily armed, paramilitary "detectives" knocking on your door and questioning you about your involvement with the United Mine Workers of America, the UMWA. And, if you didn't say the right words, they would threaten your eviction, or worse. In many cases, that's exactly what the mining companies did. They relied heavily on the Baldwin-Felts detective agency to enforce their wishes. How could this be remotely legal? Not just civil rights were ignored, but human rights as well. Such an unequal balance of power could only last for so long.

Matewan miners working for the Stone Mountain Coal Co. Circa 1920. Photo complements of a life-long citizen of Matewan. Notice the mules. These beasts were commonly used to pull the coal from the mines.

It was bad enough that federal labor laws were virtually non-existent. But an equally significant concern of the miners was safety, or the lack thereof. Think of the 1980 musical hit "Canary in a Coal Mine," by the English band, The Police. That song would never have been written had the minors not discovered that a canary will die from methane gas well before a human will. The mining companies took full advantage of the sparse regulations of the time. Federal regulations to protect the well-being of the average worker were either in a developmental stage, or non-existent. It depended on the industry.

The miners were forced to develop their own methods to survive, and they did. They had many experiences to remind them of the dangers of mining coal. If you counted the ethnicity of the greatest number of miners killed, the Italians are at the top of this list. Of the following mining disasters in West Virginia, in the early 20th century, most were caused by careless employees that dismissed the accepted mining practices of the time. However, both the miners and the owners played a role. As with most everything in life, blame is a four-lane highway. Unfortunately, the victims of these disasters passed onto the next life and many remain nameless.

The worst mining disaster in American history happened in Marion County, WV. It was in the small town of Monongah in December 1907. An estimated 362--367 miners died, almost instantly, from a series of blasts so large its effects were felt as far away as eight miles. Some miners were simply "vaporized" and were never found. Most of them were Italian immigrants. There is still a vibrant Italian community in Northern West Virginia today. Other WV mining disasters include the Eccles mine near Beckley, WV in April 1914. Between 174 and 186 miners died. In the small Fayette County town of Layland, in March 1915, approximately 115 miners died. In April 1924, in Marshall County, near Wheeling, WV, the Benwood mining disaster took the lives of 119 miners. And, in April 1927, in Everettville, WV, near Morgantown, that mine disaster killed between 109 and 111 miners. The total death toll from just these five mining disasters killed somewhere between 879 and 898 miners. Just about all of them had families. They all occurred inside a 20-year time frame. In each disaster, methane gas was the root cause. There were many other tragedies just as horrific. These five examples simply represent the ones with the highest number of casualties within a 20-year snapshot of our history. Aside from these disasters, many more would die from "pneumoconiosis," otherwise known as black lung.

From blasting processes, to roof support standards, ventilation and drainage processes, even bringing birds into your workspace, the early coal miners helped establish the foundations of the modern safety standards we understand today. The companies that employed these people unwittingly forced them to become entrepreneurs and engineers because they (the employers) didn't care that much about safety. Certainly, they cared less than the average miner did. It was very much life and death for the average coal miner in this time. Mining safety innovations were pioneered by the miner more than the employer. Even the creation of the U. S. Bureau of Mines in 1910 did little to advance the safety of the miners. That agency did assist the states with mine inspections, but their primary focus was research of mining methods (and disasters) and disseminating their findings to states and other agencies in the government. I'm not saying this agency wasn't helpful, but many thousands of miners (from all types of mining) lost their lives between 1910 and the dismantling of the bureau in 1996. The early coal miners in West Virginia looked after their own safety more than the government did. And, certainly more than the mining companies did.

∽ The Adversaries Evolve ∽

The best stories almost always feature a good guy and a bad guy. Usually, the bad guy starts trouble with the good guy. As the conflict escalates, a fierce battle eventually takes place. When it looks like the bad guy is just about to win, the good guy finds some superpower he didn't know he had. Sometimes, he gets help from a superhuman ally to win the day. Unfortunately, this story is not like that. It's more of a story about a bad guy and a worse bad guy. To muddle it ever further, the worse bad guy was actually two guys, and they had an army. They were fierce businessmen who valued the completion of a contract more than the human consequences of their wake.

As was common in this era, the downtrodden had to choose between the lesser of two evils. It was a harsh and dismal place filled with daring and rugged people. For many, it was their first few years in America. It was nothing like the society we understand today because it was more than complicated. So, to make it easier, there will be a good guy and there will be a bad guy. The good guy was Sid Hatfield. The bad guy was William G. Baldwin and Thomas A. Felts. William and Thomas owned and managed the Baldwin-Felts Detective Agency. They employed an army of "detectives." There were hundreds of them, and they were all fierce warriors.

Sid Hatfield and the Baldwin-Felts Detective Agency are the main players in this story. But, the really, really bad guys were the coal mining companies. Sid, William, and Thomas were only reacting to the environment created by the owners and investors who were controlled by laws that allowed this to happen. As unscrupulous as they were, these purveyors of terror actually played by the rules. This is the "atom splitting" realization. That these unlikely forces would come to meet on the battlefield of civility is pretty big. The consequences for all American workers would be impacted by this turbulence. The final victor would not be known until many years later, but the right thing would eventually happen.

In the era of 1918 to 1920, the second industrial revolution was winding down. The roaring 20's was taking shape. In the background, after the bloodbath of World War 1, death was somewhat devalued. 1920 was also nearing the end of the horrible influenza pandemic, colloquially known as the Spanish Flu. This pandemic is responsible for the death of somewhere between three and five percent of the world population at the time. To put it another way, it's estimated that 50 million people died worldwide from this flu between 1918 and 1920. Some estimates go as high as 100 million. Combine that with 16 million soldiers who died in World War 1 and you can see why virtually everyone in American was affected by the death of someone they knew and loved.

The mining companies didn't create these circumstances, nor the economics of the time. They simply saw a need and they tried to fill it. It was a time of tremendous new opportunity to make money. They operated inside the laws of the time, and those times were booming. Did they take advantage of the proletariat masses? Yes they did. Unfortunately, that's the darker side of human nature. Sid was a small spoke in a much larger wheel. But every great fire begins with the smallest spark. The spark was Sid's endorsement of the miner's unionization effort. The gasoline was Baldwin-Felts contract to prevent the formation of a union, however they saw fit. And all the while, the black gold flowed seamlessly from the valleys and hollows of West Virginia.

Oliver S. Beckette. U.S. Army infantry. Company A, 315th Regiment, 80th Rainbow Division. Field Artillery. 1918. He spent 52 days on the German front line. Discharged Private, First Class in 1918. He survived the Spanish Flu and the German machine guns of France. He fought 52 days at St. Mihiel, Argonne. A French family helped him recover from the flu during a two month period. He lived to be 87 and died of natural causes in Ona, WV. He is my grandfather.

Who Was Sid?

Sid Hatfield was born in Blackberry, Kentucky in 1893. However, some of my research places his birth in 1891. Either way, that would make him very close to 30 years old when he arrived in Welch, West Virginia on August 1st, 1921. Sid Hatfield was both a hero and a villain. But most of all, he was a fighter. His thin and slight body, just 5' 4" tall, was always underestimated by his enemies. He won almost every battle until his ultimate death. Sid Hatfield had a significant impact on the modern working conditions of the average American today.

"Smilin' Sid" (his legendary name) was a champion for the poorest of poor coal miners in Southern West Virginia in the early 20th century. He was a law enforcement officer and also an outlaw, depending on who you ask. He was a hard drinking, hard living, no nonsense commoner who was both adored and despised in his community. He grew up fast and hard, like most of the survivors in this time and place. He was hated by the coal mining companies and the politicians aligned with them. Sid Hatfield was a resident of Mingo County, WV, but he was not born there, and he did not die there. He is not buried there, either.

The son of Jacob and Rebecca Hatfield, he was one of 12 children. He was born just a few years after the legendary Hatfield and McCoy feud ended. Sid's father was a tenant farmer. His family worked a hardscrabble farm in Blackberry, which is in Pike County, Kentucky, just over the Tug Fork River from Matewan. Of Jacob & Rebecca's 12 children, nine survived beyond childhood.

Sid Hatfield's grave in the Buskirk, KY cemetery. It's a steep and narrow drive to get there from the Tug, but it's not far. Just ask the locals, they'll tell you where it is. (That's what I did) This picture was taken in May, 2019. Just like May 19th, 1920, almost 100 years ago, it was a warm and humid day. There were off and on showers. It was a typical Spring day on the Tug.

From a very early age, Sid had to work. He first worked for his family, then as a coal miner and later as a blacksmith. These were all backbreaking occupations that would sculpt anyone's body. Sid Hatfield was young and fit when he accepted the job of chief of police in the small town of Matewan. Not only was he smart, but everyone knew his bite would sting. They also knew he had their back. This new job would prove to be just as challenging as his previous jobs. But Sid's rough and tumble nature was quickly replaced by the legal necessity of his new role.

View from a cedar grove on the North side of the Buskirk cemetery. A brief but strong downpour made me duck under this hammock while searching for Sid's grave. My feet were soaked. I didn't pack an umbrella. I didn't plan well. This was typical Matewan weather in May, 1920.

As chief of police, and a leader in his community, winning a fist fight in a local bar was quite unfavorable to his new career. He gained the trust of the common citizen by showing them leadership and giving them hope. Before Sid, there was nothing like this. He stood up to the overwhelming power of the time. Sid Hatfield was the Rosa Parks to the citizens of Matewan. Only, it was worse than the segregated

South. There were no Jim Crow laws in Matewan. There never were any. Everyone who opposed their employer was oppressed, viciously and equally. Sid Hatfield was the only one who went "all in." He captured the soul of Matewan and maybe the entire region. He was daring enough to attract the attention of the cigar-smoking top hats in far away places. I wonder if he knew that.

Sid's teeth (most of them) were capped with gold and this feature had much to do with his nickname, Smiling Sid. He was also known as "Two Gun Sid." He was known to carry a police .38 revolver and a Smith & Wesson .44 revolver. This is a picture of his SW.44. You can view this

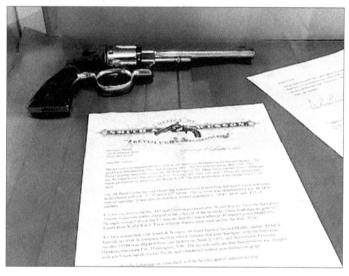

Sid Hatfield's Smith & Wesson .44 revolver. Complements of the Matewan Welcome Center. Sid did not use this weapon in the Matewan Massacre. He obtained it later. I'm pretty convinced he left this pistol in his hotel room, in Welch, WV, on August 1st, 1921.

gun at the Matewan Welcome Center and museum on the down-river side of town. It's well worth the visit. It's a super cool museum.

Sid was frugal, self-reliant, and smart. He could charm a rattle snake and then eat it for dinner. He would back down to no one, at any time, for any reason. This characteristic, however, may have been his greatest weakness. Those who followed him, followed him hard.

Those that did not, learned to at least take him very seriously. Everyone knew he had a weapon on him at all times. Everyone knew Sid Hatfield was quite capable of pulling the trigger. Everyone knew Sid was committed to the cause of the miners and to some form of justice. I imagine they loved him as much as they feared him. He was no-nonsense, and no one doubted that. But somehow, he smiled a lot. His trademark was his smile. His gold-plated teeth were common, but not always prevalent at the time. A good dentist in 1920 was quite expensive. Not many people could afford to have their teeth fixed.

When Sid Hatfield moved to Matewan, sometime in his late teens or early twenties, the town had only three avenues and maybe 10 streets. (Honestly, it still does.) Through the center of the town's buildings, there was a consistently muddy road known as Main Street. Behind that, along the railroad tracks, was Mate Street. Mate street was named after the pioneer founder's dog, "Mate," who was eaten by a bear, in the 1700's. In 1920, between the railway depot on one side of town and the mayor's office on the other side of town, you could get a haircut, something to eat, get your shoes repaired, or buy new ones. You could gamble, get a drink, pay your taxes, or purchase any number of essential foods or tools. (Sorry, no lotto tickets were available during this time). You could also mail a letter, buy a book, or even buy a nice cigar. Matewan was an oasis of civilization among the mountains of nothing. 100 years ago, all of the buildings were modern, thriving, and exciting. But it was all controlled by an elite handful. There were no roads leading into or out of this town. The only way you could get there was by rail or horseback. This was a remote boom town that rivaled the stories of the old West. It was classic. The very few had complete control over the very many, and revolt was about to engulf the entire region. But, to the newcomer, it was certainly shiny and exciting. It was a boom town

Even though there were very few roads in Matewan, the wealthy citizens were still able to import the Ford Model T. Featured here is R. W. Buskirk on the left. He was a prominent citizen in Matewan and a significant building was named after him. The name of the young boy is unknown. Possibly his son.

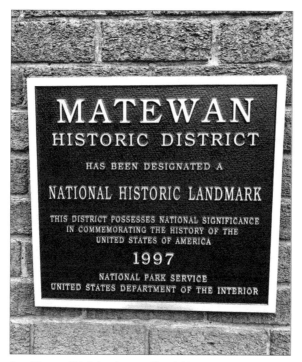

One of the many historical markers you will see in Matewan.

Near the intersection of Hwy 52, (King Coal Hwy) and Rte 65. Red Jacket, WV. It's about four miles to Matewan from here. This highway is an engineering marvel. Hopefully, you can see why there were no roads into Matewan in 1920. The mountains simply did not permit the access we enjoy today.

Sid Hatfield's apartment in Matewan was upstairs in the Nenni building. Notice the raised sidewalk. This is a common characteristic of many small towns in the mountains of WV. Richwood WV is another great example. Sid's front door is on the far left. He lived on the 2nd floor.

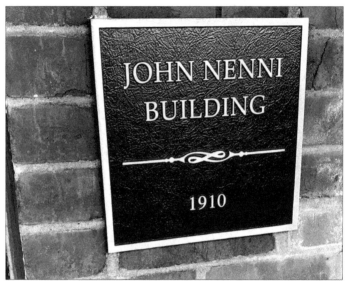

The John Nenni building historical marker in present day Matewan.

MOURNING citizens of Matewan and elsewhere stand in line on the town's main stree[t] while waiting to ascend the stairs to the apartment of Matewan's slain police chief, Sid Hatfield, who with Ed Chambers, was shot from ambush and killed on the courthouse s[teps] Welch. (Photo courtesy of Kerry Burmeister)

The John Nenni building in August, 1921. Many, many thanks to Kathi Sherrell for this pic. Super nice person. The raised sidewalk is clear to see. This "viewing" was significant, but the funeral produced an even greater crowd. My research shows over 2,000 citizens attended the funeral, in a driving rain.

I cannot say for sure what occupation Sid Hatfield held upon his arrival to Matewan, but he soon found sway with the mayor, Cabell Cornelious Testerman. They were very close in age. They were both young. Sid Hatfield and Cabell Testerman were both pro-union organizers, and they found great benefit in becoming allies. Cabell had legislative power, and Sid had physical power. Cabell was a politician, and Sid was a community organizer. Cabell hired Sid Hatfield to become the chief of police for Matewan. One side of the ticket had a way with words. The other side had a way with guns. They quickly became the best of friends. They would rule for at least two years in Matewan. Whatever Sid expected when he moved to Matewan, I believe he exceeded that goal.

Sid Hatfield would not get married until the death of his best friend, the mayor of Matewan, Cabell Cornelis Testerman. Mr. Testerman died in the Matewan Massacre. (More on that soon.) Sid's marriage was short-lived. Mayor Testerman was a union supporter, like Sid, and therefore an enemy of the mining companies. Cabell asked Sid Hatfield to look after his wife and child should he be killed. This type of agreement among desperados was fairly common in these times. Jessie Testerman had a young son with Cornelis. His name was Jackson. It may be that Sid Hatfield simply honored his best friend's wishes and married Jessie Testerman and (possibly) adopted Jackson. On the other hand, it may be that Sid was already in love with Jessie, or maybe it was vice versa. Either way, I bet they had the most thrilling year of marriage. It was action packed, to say the least.

The Baldwin-Felts agency claimed Mr. Testerman was killed by Sid Hatfield. Their evidence was supported by the speed in which he married Jessie, just two weeks later. I asked a local historian, Eric Simons, if he believed this was true, and he said no. I'm inclined to agree with Eric, but the real truth will probably elude our history. Sid Hatfield and Jessie Testerman were married in Huntington, West Virginia on June 2nd, 1920. They were married for about 14 months before he was murdered by detective Charlie E. Lively. Jessie Maynard Hatfield, twice inside 15 months, was a widow again. Both of her husbands were shot and killed by Baldwin-Felts detectives.

ᓚ Bloodlines ᓚ

Sid Hatfield was distantly related to William Anderson "Devil Anse" Hatfield. Devil Anse was the patriarch of the Hatfield side of the renowned feud. He was a Captain in the Confederate Army. The following pictures include his grave in Crystal Block, WV. The Hatfield family cemetery is about 30 miles north of Matewan on Hwy 44, in Logan County. Also known as the Jerry West Hwy., the Hatfield Cemetery is just a few miles south of Omar, WV. It's a bit of a rough ride from Logan to Rte. 52 in Mingo County. There are active coal mines dotted along this route. These mountains would not see the thousands of miners marching toward Matewan in 1922. They were stopped near Logan by federal reserve troops from the U.S. Army. Nor would they see miners from Matewan marching toward Logan. They would have been cast into the wilderness at a minimum, and many would have been shot, at worst. Either way, they just couldn't leave the town to protest. This parcel of West Virginia remained relatively peaceful during this turbulent time. With all the destruction to the North and South of this nook of Earth, maybe it's well this warrior was able to rest in eternal peace.

Sid Hatfield's great grandfather was Jeremiah Hatfield. Jeremiah was a half-brother to Valentine Hatfield, 1789-1867. Valentine Hatfield was the grandfather of Devil Anse. Best I can figure, they were half grandsons. During the tumultuous era of early 20th century Appalachia, bloodlines really mattered. Say what you want, but they still do. I believe Sid Hatfield had just enough Devil Anse blood in him to help gain the trust of the beleaguered miners. They knew Devil Anse was an honorable man, and a deeply religious person. They also knew he was very capable of killing. It's very possible the people of Matewan associated Sid's actions (what they witnessed) with the capabilities of a distant relative named Devil Anse. Many may disagree, but Captain

Cap't William Anderson Hatfield. "Devil Anse." Picture complements of the Hatfield McCoy House bed & breakfast in Williamson, WV. An affordable night's stay and a history lesson for free. He fought for the Confederates in the Civil War. Even though he officially left the "cause" in 1863, he continued to fight for Confederacy. He formed his own militia and remained active until his Amnesty Oath on May 4th, 1865.

"Devil Anse" Anderson was a very moral man, even though he was willing to use violence to defend his cause. If so, it may explain the majority support in Sid's community. The people needed someone capable of changing their whole dynamic. They needed someone who would take the risks they weren't able (or willing) to take. Sid was their guy.

Historic marker on WV Rte 44 between Logan and Matewan, WV. A.k.a. The Jerry West Highway.

Cap't William Anderson Hatfield "Devil Anse" grave site. Notice all the coins placed at the foot of his memorial. The stone was imported from Italy.

If you want to see the Devil Anse gravesite, be prepared for a steep and rocky incline of about 200 feet in elevation. You may get winded, but it's well worth it. This is great American history that is still available to everyone, for free. But please, pack it in, pack it out.

Let's Continue with William

William Gibboney Baldwin was born in Tazewell Co. VA in May 1860. He died in March 1936 in Roanoke, VA. He was the oldest of five brothers and four sisters. His parents were Dennison B. Baldwin and Sallie Barns Baldwin. There is little documentation about his childhood, except that he enjoyed reading. He read dime store detective novels and soon became interested in that type of work. It was a perfectly legal occupation in those days. Yet, it was a dangerous and risky profession, so I'm fairly sure that kind of job excited him. In 1884, he found employment with the Eureka Detective Agency in Charleston, WV. Shortly thereafter, he met and married Katherine English. They had two sons. Sadly, they separated sometime in the early 1890's and William moved to Roanoke, VA. It is then and there he founded his legendary company. He named it Baldwin's Railroad Detectives.

William had a brother-in-law named William Jackson Jenks. He was the general manager, and later vice president, of the Norfolk & Western Railroad. Naturally, Mr. Baldwin secured a contract to protect the interests of this railroad in Western Virginia, Southern West Virginia and Eastern Kentucky. This would be the very heart of coal country, then and now. From an investor's standpoint, it was like buying stock in a shovel manufacturing company after gold was discovered at Sutter's Mill. The railroad companies were expanding new lines into new valleys at a super hasty pace, and cost. They were hiring laborers from all over the planet. Baldwin's agency helped to maintain a continuous operation in the region. He deterred train robberies, internal theft, and interestingly, controlled the supervision of the railroad's labor force. In this regard, I believe he was paid to ensure that no union would be able to establish a foothold with the railroad workers, and predictively, the mine workers. I believe this became the primary motivation throughout the remainder of his career. He was paid to suppress union formation. I hate to say it, but he was good at it. He was like a human resources director with a pistol. By chance or design, William Baldwin would soon meet another businessman, significantly compatible with his needs, known as Thomas L. Felts.

Power Expands

Since the "detective agency" business was perfectly legal during this time, you might expect some sort of government oversight. There was some, but it was very limited. This was an emerging industry with negligible regulatory precedent. There weren't a lot of rules at the time. The detectives were actually duly sworn officers of the law. They were appointed as sheriffs by an elected judge. Many were deactivated soldiers from WW1. Most were really good with horses. Some were marksmen. Some knew how to cook food in extreme circumstances. Some were good at predicting an opponent's next move. Regardless, the Baldwin-Felts Detective Agency only hired people capable of meeting their needs. They hired skilled workers. On the other hand, the mining companies preferred unskilled workers. It was a classic imbalance of power. Not only that, Balwin-Felts had access to weapons that far exceeded the small arms of the miners.

William Baldwin basically wrote the rules for the detective industry. Right or wrong, he blazed a trail. Federal oversight was only incumbent on local, "elected" law enforcement, but only them. Due to the sparse population and the impossible terrain, most county sheriffs and their deputies were unable to provide basic security to many remote areas. They just didn't have the manpower, or the roads, or the time. As a result, they were forced to deputize employees (private citizens) into a legitimate protection agency. The detectives would swear an oath in the nearest courthouse, get their badge, and vamoose. However, they would ultimately report to William Gibboney Baldwin, one way or another. For the most part, he wrote their paycheck.

He was a self-made man that found his riches through hard work and sheer determination. His rise to fortune was both common and accepted in this era. He became a local investor and philanthropist in and around Roanoke, VA. He lived the American dream and found satisfaction and wealth doing what he loved. However, he was also no stranger to violence. He faced many showdowns before his death. As a detective, he pulled his trigger many times. He shot and killed at least one person during a "legal" police action in Virginia. He had bullets fired at him as well. He was also a severe racist, in my opinion. There are examples to support this thesis.

In a racially charged event in 1898, William G Baldwin shot and killed an African American man in Petersburg, Virginia. He was working as a detective and attempting to make an arrest. The details of this event are unclear. He claimed he was defending himself against 14 men when he fired his weapon. Ultimately, he was acquitted by a jury. The verdict was self-defense. (It happened a lot during the era.)

In 1893, he arrested Thomas Smith, also an African-American male from Roanoke, Virginia. Thomas was being held as a suspect in the rape of a local white woman. When a protest gathered outside the jail in Roanoke, William G. Baldwin refused to help city officials protect Thomas Smith, and a riot soon ensued. Mr. Smith was lynched and killed.

In 1904, Baldwin intervened in the case of another African American male accused of assault on another white woman, also from Roanoke. The suspect, Henry Williams, claimed at trial that Baldwin made a visit to his jail cell and got him drunk. He claimed Baldwin extracted a confession to the crime and (probably) leaked the news to the community. At trial, Mr. Williams claimed he was coerced into a confession. Another mob attempted to lynch Mr. Williams. This time the suspect was protected. Baldwin had a lot of local influence in Roanoke by now. Mr. Williams survived just long enough to be hanged for the alleged crime, due (most likely) to the coerced confession. William Gibboney Baldwin thrived in these violent times. He was a pragmatic and effective businessman willing to achieve his personal goals by any means necessary. He was certainly determined, but not so much constrained.

I believe Sid Hatfield was an unwitting pawn of the inevitable conflict between our modern labor practices and the harsh labor practices of the early 20th century. He was brave enough to stand up to the powerful Baldwin-Felts Detective Agency. But he was naive enough to think he could win. In this part of Appalachia, during this time, gunfights, shootouts, and murder were common. Neither Sid Hatfield nor the Baldwin Felts Detective Agency was a stranger to this violence. It's a hard leap, but I believe this agency created Sid Hatfield more than he created himself. They absolutely hated him.

Most federal law enforcement agents didn't have the capacity to maintain civil order during this great unrest. The void was created by the harsh geography and the lack of infrastructure. Appalachia was rugged and mostly undeveloped. There were few roads and few options to get from point A to point B. Deputized "detectives" were legal and thus authorized to use lethal force if necessary. Our federal government was hamstrung by the lack of resources, or maybe interests, to regulate such a private police force. Honestly, with all the expansion and world conflict going on, this region was hardly a priority. Consider, in 1920, both Arizona and New Mexico had joined the union only eight years prior. And yet, pockets of the Wild West were still common in parts of the East. The oversight and modernization of law enforcement was still about 20 years away at this time. If you were a small-town police chief in Appalachia, you were basically on your own. You also had great discretion on how you handled civil unrest within your jurisdiction. As the new federal laws were being written, Sid was just trying to help his people.

William Baldwin's main client was the Norfolk & Western Railroad. He became their "chief special agent," and he held that position until his retirement in 1930. He was paid to execute the desires of his clients. And, like any business, he would only get paid if he produced the desired results. William G. Baldwin worked within the legal boundaries of his time. However, those legal boundaries were far different than what they are today. The coal mining companies of the early 20th century enjoyed a lack of federal oversight that would be unthinkable today. William G Baldwin found a niche in what is basically the "protection industry." And, he found it at the perfect time.

Sid Hatfield didn't care about any of that. He probably had no concept that he would ultimately change the entire game for the hourly worker in America. He only cared about his community and their suffering. I imagine he enjoyed the power of public office. I suspect it was intoxicating to his nature. The Baldwin-Felts agents were only doing what their primary customer desired. That primary customer, in Matewan, was the Stone Mountain Coal Company, and they soon became contemptuous of Sid Hatfield. They urged Mr. Baldwin to address the developing situation, but he had different fish to fry. So he delegated the Sid Hatfield issue to his loyal partner, Thomas Lafayette Felts. T. L. Felts had two brothers, Albert and Lee, and they would soon meet Sid Hatfield.

A Bit About Thomas

Thomas Lafayette Felts was born in Galax, Virginia on October 16, 1868. He died in a hotel in Richmond, Virginia on September 9th, 1937, at the age of 69. According to the Bluefield Daily Telegraph, he suffered a stroke. It was also reported he battled heart disease. He was a two term State Senator for the state of Virginia. He was also a lawyer and a member of the Virginia BAR Association. Whereas Baldwin specialized in the railroad side of the agency, Thomas Felts handled the mining company side of the business. Throughout his career as a detective, he was involved in at least 20 shootouts. During one such gun fight, he was shot in the chest with a .45 caliber pistol. Although he almost bled to death, the bullet didn't injure any vital organs and he survived. Like Sid Hatfield and William Baldwin, he was a super tough dude. He was quite the adversary.

In 1900, he joined the Baldwin Detective Agency. His allure to William Baldwin was, probably, the enhancement of professional legal advice for a young company that was growing in both size and controversy. In 1910, Thomas Felts was made a full partner in the agency. The company was renamed the Baldwin-Felts Detective Agency and Thomas now owned 50 percent of this nascent, sleuth organization. Thomas Felts had to do some heavy stuff to be considered for employment by Mr Baldwin, let alone be promoted to a full partner. I believe both of these businessmen were super tough hombres who were not easily intimidated by danger.

They founded their headquarters in Bluefield, West Virginia, and later in Roanoke, Virginia. The company's original purpose was to support the investigation of train robberies, among other crimes committed against the emerging railroad companies in Appalachia. But like everything in the world of business, circumstances change. The railroad companies were intrinsically connected to the coal mining companies and therefore mutually linked to the production of bituminous coal in Southern Appalachia. Neither the rail companies, nor the mining companies, or the detective agencies (employed by both), cared much about how the coal was produced. And, as mentioned, there was little oversight (federal or state) regarding the labor practices of the coal companies. They all had deadlines to meet and quotas to fill. It was just business.

The investors, then as today, expected favorable numbers. Disruptions from the union were considered a serious threat to their mutual interest. There became a legitimate business need for a "paid" police force to protect the interests of the companies. The emerging squabble was perfectly suited for the Baldwin-Felts Detective Agency. Right or wrong, these events set the stage for the 1920 show-down in Matewan, and beyond ... well beyond.

It Started With a Kiss

Probably the most spectacular achievement during Thomas's detective career was the apprehension and arrest of Floyd Allen in 1912, as well as other members of the Allen clan following a massive manhunt. Floyd Allen was a prominent land owner and businessman in Carroll County, Virginia. He was influential in local politics and a strong democratic party supporter. However, he had many scuffles with law enforcement throughout his life. He bore the wounds of 13 bullets, one of which was to his chest. Five of the weapons that struck him were fired by a member of his own family. Somehow, he survived each incident. Somehow, he always managed to find legal recourse from conviction. He was very well connected to local law enforcement and the local judiciary. Most of his previous arrests were for violent acts such as assault and battery. He owned a profitable general store, ran a moonshine operation and even dabbled as a local sheriff. His sway and swagger always managed to keep him out of jail. The episodes of 1912, however, proved that his pride went too far. That edge of civility was a courthouse shootout on March 14, 1912 in Hillsville, VA. It was a bloodbath with five casualties and seven wounded.

It all started when Floyd Allen was arrested for interfering with the lawful apprehension of his nephews, Sidna Allen and Westley Edwards. They were charged with making a public disturbance at a local church. It was during a corn shucking bee in Hillsville, VA , on a Saturday night, in December 1910. (Some sources say it was in 1911). Allegedly, Westley Edwards kissed a young girl who was romantically tied to another local youth named Will Thomas. Unfortunately, this event led to an altercation between the Allen clan and the Thomas family. Murder and violence were regrettably common in this place, at this time. But, so too was chivalry. As I see it, the event must have been a social crisis in this small, Southern town where everyone knew everyone. Floyd Allen had great influence in this community, but he was soon challenged by the actions of his own family. I bet he was really, really pissed about an incident that was created by his immediate family members. It was an incident that would ultimately cause him to be executed in the electric chair.

The day after the "incident," Sunday morning, during local church services, Will Thomas called out Westley Edwards to a fight. I have no idea what words he used. But, Will had three of his friends with him. I imagine this event took place in the front lawn of the church, but I can't say with certainty. Young Mr. Thomas whipped his friends into a fury prior to the event. These rivals were from two of the most influential families in Hillsville. Their ruckus affected more than just themselves. It affected the whole community.

The assault on the young Westley, by Thomas and his three friends, was probably swift and violent. I can envision the congregation scattering toward the perimeter of the church property as the assault began. It was a big commotion. Westley's brother, Sidna, saw the attack happening and quickly raced to his brother's defense. The fight was on, and it was four against two. It must have been crazy. I have nothing to back this up, but I can see Sidna ripping into Will Thomas with a fury as he joined the altercation--probably at a full speed run. He probably pummeled Will with a fusillade of fists to the face and upper body. I imagine Will's friends quickly realized they chose the wrong dudes to fight. However, because the charges against the Edwards brothers included disorderly conduct, assault with a deadly weapon and disturbing a public worship service, I think the Allen brothers wacked their opponents and then pulled out a pistol and issued final threats. I think it's safe to say, the rich kids messed with the kids from the other side of the tracks.

Westley and Sidna fled the state of Virginia to avoid arrest soon after this altercation. They left for North Carolina, specifically, Surry County. This is the county that would make the Andy Griffith Show famous some 50 years later. Soon after, they both found employment with a local granite quarry. Given the Allen family's history, I imagine they were pretty smug for having skirted the law. But, the Deputy Clerk of Carroll Co. Virginia, Dexter Goad, soon issued warrants for Westley and Sidna's arrest and notified the sheriff of Surry Co., NC. The brothers were arrested and scheduled to return to Hillsville, VA. When Floyd Allen learned of these events, he allowed his emotions to launch a chain reaction of unfavorable events for him. Floyd Allen's beef with the arrest and extradition was basically this; he claimed the state (of Virginia) did not obtain proper requisition papers from the governor of Virginia

Modern day Hillsville, VA. Super cool little town. Awesome history. Shopping and restaurants abound. This view is directly across from the Courthouse. Notice the last building on the far right. More on that shortly.

to cross state lines and make the arrest. So, on the return trip to Carroll Co. VA, Westley and Sidna Edwards were restrained in a horse drawn buggy that was driven by Hillsville deputy Thomas F. Samuel, and the owner of the buggy, Peter Easter. (He was also a deputy. Think of an old Western Stagecoach team, only, it was a buckboard.) Westley Edwards had a history of trying to escape so he was handcuffed to the front seat of the buggy beside the owner, Peter Easter. Sidna was tied-up in the back seat beside deputy Thomas Samuel. Unfortunately, the deputy only brought one pair of handcuffs for this extradition. He had to restrain Sidna in the back of the buggy with hemp rope.

As they moved ever closer toward the courthouse in Hillsville, VA, they passed by several properties owned by the Allen family. Floyd was probably riding nearby, watching and waiting. On one such property, near his brother's home, Floyd Allen obstructed the coach by blocking the road with his horse. It was a narrow stretch of road with no other path. (There weren't many roads to choose from at this time.) After being blocked with no other option to proceed, Thomas Samuel demanded Floyd Allen move out of the way, or else. After Floyd refused multiple times, Mr. Samuel found the courage to pull out his revolver, (my guess a .38), point it at Floyd Allen, and pull the trigger.

Unfortunately for the deputy, the gun proved to be inoperable. It either misfired because of defective ammo, or maybe it was just a bad revolver. This was the golden age of the six-shot revolver, but their mass production made their reliability suspect, depending on the manufacturer. Everywhere in Europe, New England USA, not to mention South American countries, they were producing these weapons by the millions. Therefore, many of these weapons were unreliable. Colt, Remington, Smith & Wesson, and of course John Browning, introduced the semi-automatic handgun to America. It's very unlikely Mr. Samuels had the latest gun innovation. I don't think Floyd did either.

The proliferation of the semi-automatic handgun was just beginning to sweep the nation in 1912. It was very new and completely different from the revolver. They were very reliable and super accurate. They still are. John Browning was well ahead of the curve in 1911. He invented the semi-auto .45 handgun that was the gold standard of the time, and it still is. But they weren't cheap. Mr. Samuel did not own this type of weapon. Not many people did. I doubt Floyd did as well. I don't think it mattered what type of weapon Floyd had, if he even had a weapon at all. He was focused on bringing his nephews home, regardless of the circumstances.

Floyd rode around the wagon, slowly, then dismounted his horse and boarded Samuel's carriage. After a brief fight, Floyd was able to remove the pistol from Samuel and use it to beat him nearly to death. Floyd pistol whipped Thomas Samuel, a duly sworn deputy from Carroll County Virginia, with his own gun. Floyd Allen left Mr. Samuel half dead after the altercation. He threw him into a ditch, face down, unconscious. And, just to be a total jerk, he ran off Samuel's horses. Floyd collected his nephews and began to take them home. As Peter Easter fled the scene, he stopped, turned around, fired a few rounds at Floyd. One round struck Floyd in the finger. I don't know which finger, but it was just one more gunshot wound to Floyd. He had many others already. Unfortunately, this would not be the final gun fight in the life of Floyd Allen.

Floyd Gets His

The Carroll County District Attorney for the Virginia Commonwealth was William Foster. He was elected as Carroll County's prosecutor on the Democratic ticket and had served under that capacity for eight years. However, preceding the next election, he switched parties to the Republican side and won reelection. His opponent was Walter Allen, the son of the local Constable, Jack Allen. In a complete reversal of friendship, Floyd Allen and William Foster became bitter rivals. Floyd was a diehard Democrat. In this election, the Democratic contender lost a fiercely contested election, and thus the Republicans won. This must have been very personal to Floyd Allen. To further infuriate him, he would now be prosecuted by a former ally and political intimate. Basically, he was very likely to be convicted by a former best friend.

Before the trial of Floyd Allen, both Sidna and Westley were convicted, and both were sentenced to 30 and 60 days respectively for the fight at the church. Both served their sentence on work release. In essence, they escaped justice. The way I see it, this consequence only promoted future violent behavior from these determined and serious men. Pride, esteem, and social position was legally challenged. The social order of many years was disrupted in this small community. A gun fight was sadly inevitable.

Floyd Allen went to his trial on March 13th, 1912, at the Hillsville, VA. courthouse. His two-team attorneys were Walter Tipton and David Bolen—both former judges in Carroll County. However, the state's case against Floyd Allen was strong and he knew it. There were many witnesses called and much testimony given. Imagine a deeply divided community regarding Floyd Allen's reputation and his history. He had many political allies and just as many foes. He had long used threats and intimidation to maintain his power and status. He was known for his violent behavior and no one doubted his capacity to follow through with his threats.

Carroll County Courthouse in Hillsville, VA. Built in 1872, it remained the seat of government until 1998. This is where the shootout happened on March 14, 1912

There were rumors among the citizens of Hillsville that Floyd Allen had threatened Thomas Samuel prior to the trial. Floyd found a way to communicate this message; If Thomas testified against him, he would never be found. This may be true, or maybe not. But, Deputy Samuel fled the state of Virginia the same night he received the threat. This man would have been a very key witness. As a result, the judge was forced to convene a grand jury to strengthen the state's case. The eyewitness was suddenly gone. The state was forced to rely heavily on the testimony of the other main witness, Peter Easter--the man who shot Floyd's finger.

Upon completion of the trial, the jury was unable to reach a verdict. They were sequestered in a hotel for the night. The next day, they finally reached a conclusion. Many of Floyd's family were present in the courtroom. They were certainly armed. Most of the court officials (and some of the jury members) were also armed. Metal detectors didn't exist. Judge Massie told family members he had a bad feeling about the trial. The tension in the courtroom must have been palpable. Like a pile of dry brush in October, it would only take a tiny spark to engulf the whole situation into flames. The jury finally produced the verdict of guilty and recommended one year in the state penitentiary.

Floyd Allen warned the judge, Thornton Massie, if sentenced on that verdict, "I will kill you." When ordered to rise, he stood up slowly. Witnesses say he wobbled at first, but soon gained his composure. Before the jury foreman could sit down, the judge immediately sentenced Floyd Allen to one year in the penitentiary in Richmond, VA. Floyd Allen snapped at this moment. He began moving toward the bench, at first slowly, then quickly. The courthouse was small and filled to capacity (maybe 50 people). Accounts say that Floyd Allen was so enraged he was almost unable to speak. I have no doubt he was also well armed at this moment. He finally exclaimed to Judge Massie, "I ain't a going!" and continued to rush the bench.

Exactly who fired the first shot will forever be in dispute. However, a fierce and deadly shootout developed with many shooters involved. Imagine your neighbors and fellow citizens whipping out a pistol at a civil court proceeding and the gun fire came from the jury box, the congregation, and even the bench. Basically, bullets came from everywhere. More than 50 rounds were recovered during the following investigation. That shootout left the judge, Thornton L Massie, sheriff Lew F. Webb, the state attorney William Foster, and jury foreman Augustus Fowler, all dead. Also killed was a subpoenaed, 19-year-old witness, named Elizabeth Ayers. This young lady was at the trial only because she had to be. She was shot in the back while fleeing the shootout and died the next day in her own home. She had testified against Floyd Allen.

During the shootout, Floyd Allen was wounded in the hip, his thigh, and his knee, but he managed to escape the courthouse with his brother Sidna, Friel Allen and Claude Allen, and the Edwards brothers. Witnesses said all of them were participants in the shootout. As they fled the courthouse, they continued to fire their weapons. Floyd Allen escaped to the local hotel. That was as far as he could go. Westley Edwards and his uncle, Sidna Allen, fled Virginia for the state of Iowa the next day. The day after that, Floyd Allen was arrested and taken into custody. (It is my assumption he was arrested in the Hillmont Hotel because he was so severely wounded.) On his way to the

Currently named Hillmont Mercantile, this building was the Hillmont Hotel in 1912. There is some controversy as to whether this was the place Floyd Allen fled to after the shootout. I believe he did because the escape from there was much more possible than the other hotel in town. At the time, there was an open field behind this building. It would have been easy to have a horse ready to ride away from this hotel. Not so much with the other hotel.

sheriff's office, he tried to commit suicide by slashing his neck with a pocketknife but was subdued by the sheriff. He was held in the Carroll County jail until his trial. His new trial would be for murder, instead of his first trial for assault and battery. What arrogance! What a shame that so many people had to die because Floyd Allen thought he was above the law. This all happened in a US courthouse, in Virginia.

Located directly to the left of the courthouse is the Hale-Wilkerson-Carter home. If Floyd ran to this building, it would have only been about 20 yards from the courthouse. The Hillmont Hotel is about 100 yards away. Remember, he was severely wounded at this moment. According to a local resident, Steven Loutezenhiser, it is possible he ran here, but not likely. He told me, "There is not a good escape route behind this building." After being shot three times, it's an interesting theory to consider. The original structure was built in 1845 by Fielden Hale. Regardless of Floyd's escape plan, it's an impressive architecture and well worth the visit.

At the time, Virginia law was written that if a sheriff was killed, his deputies would lose all authority. Because of this technicality in the law, Carroll County had no law enforcement to pursue justice. Assistant clerk Floyd Landrith sent a telegram to the governor of Virginia, William Hodges Mann, explaining the dire situation. The governor placed a bounty on Sidna Allen ($1,000), Sidna Edwards

($1,000), Claude Allen ($800), and Friel Allen ($500). The warrant specified dead or alive. He immediately hired the Baldwin-Felts Detective Agency to track down the fugitives. T.L. Felts, (Thomas) was appointed lead detective in this case. Thomas had been a full partner in this agency for just over two years by this time. This was his opportunity to show his talent. He did not waste any time proving his skills.

As the lead investigator, Thomas quickly formed several posses. As they scoured the local countryside, they quickly discovered much of the Allen clan's hidden enterprise. Illegal moonshine stills and many gallons of moonshine were found. All of the fugitives were taken into custody within a month of the shootout, except for Westley Edwards and Sidna Allen. Thomas Felts had to travel to Iowa to track these two fugitives down. In what would be typical of this community's entanglement of order, Mr. Felts pitted one family's grievance against another to pry out clues to meet his objective. Through pure detective instincts, an informant was soon identified.

Thomas Felts likely interviewed Westley's fiancee, Maude Iroller. After a negotiated agreement, and for a sum of $500, it's believed she provided details of the location of the suspects. However, other accounts state that the father of Maude provided the location because he didn't approve of the romance and impending wedding. It is written that Maude was about to travel to Des Moines to marry Westley. I doubt this. According to local historians, the wedding was "arranged" and Maude was not in love with Westley. She may have been an opportunist and saw this as a way to earn some significant cash and also remove any doubt about her true intentions. I think she played Thomas for the money. Either way, Thomas Felts proved he was both tough and smart. As expected, he went to Iowa, found the suspects, and brought the pair back to Carroll County to face justice. From March 13, 1912, until April 15th, 1912, this event was all consuming to the American news media. It was similar to covering any major controversy today. But out of nowhere, the Titanic struck an iceberg west of Iceland. Just like that, America was done with Floyd Allen. His story was no longer front-page news. But Thomas Felts had made his name in the business. He went from nowhere to top dog in a matter of weeks. He would take this accomplishment into the mine wars of West Virginia. He was now a man that "got things done."

Ultimately, Floyd Allen was executed by electrocution on March 28th, 1913 for the crimes committed during the Hillsville courthouse shootout. Thomas Felts fulfilled his contract with the state of Virginia and secured his reputation as a "detective" that could get the job done. Say what you want about his tactics, or his character, but he became a legend for bringing closure to this tragic chapter in Southern Appalachian justice. About eight years later, his attention would be totally focused on another character.

PART 2: REDNECKS, GUNS, AND LAWYERS

About That Eight Years

Thomas L. Felts had two brothers, Albert and Lee. Both were active in the Baldwin-Felts detective agency. They played a significant role in breaking up strikes in both West Virginia and Colorado. During the Paint Creek and Cabin Creek strikes (near Charleston, WV) in 1912 and 1913, they deployed an armored railroad car with two mounted machine guns. They named it the "Death Special." These were fully automatic weapons and they fired directly into a picket line. One miner was killed, and many were wounded. This was the first time a union camp (all civilians) faced automatic gun fire. The next time was in 1914, in Colorado when the Death Special was again used to break the coal miners' strike against the Northern Coal & Coke Co. Again, several were killed and many wounded, including women and children.

In the Paint Creek, Cabin Creek and Colorado miners' strike, miners were attacked by The Baldwin-Felts agents. However, these agents were sworn officers of the law. Think about that. Can you imagine any U.S. law enforcement agency, or any proxy thereof, using automatic weapons on its own citizens because of a labor dispute? The governor of W.V., William Glasscock, commissioned a committee to investigate the tactics used by the mine guard detectives. The conclusion was that these attacks were "vicious and un-American." That's it. Nothing else happened to hold these two accountable. Albert and Lee Felts had no problem with killing innocent people. I imagine their brother Thomas felt the same.

These incidents signify the complicity of the mining companies, the railroad companies, and the West Virginia government. The rights of the miners, both civil and Constitutional, were less valuable to these entities than a shovel full of coal. As such, Sid Hatfield and his supporters were fighting both the employers and the supervisors of the employers. That's like being herded into a box canyon. Once you reach the point of no escape, you either accept your defeat, or you fight.

What Thomas Felts did in the eight years between the Floyd Allen incident and the Matewan disaster is not well documented. Much of this time was occupied by WW1 and the Spanish Flu that began near the end of the war and ended a year or so after. Also, on January 16th, 1919, the 18th Amendment to the Constitution went into effect--otherwise known as "prohibition." The Baldwin-Felts agency did not specialize in any aspect of this ruling, so it's just interesting to note. I imagine he rode out his newly found stardom doing less sensational work for the agency. But, by 1920, he would be challenged again like never before. Floyd Allen was one thing. Sid Hatfield was a much more complicated matter. Thomas Felts was up to the challenge. There's no way to prove this, but I believe William Baldwin told him to "handle it." He had other things to deal with. History was about to be made. I doubt Sid Hatfield could have known how much he would be targeted. I believe Thomas Felts was cognizant of the circumstances. The fury of chance was about to explode. We go back to Matewan.

Matewan Simmers

Throughout 1920, The mayor of Matewan, Cabell Testerman, and Sid Hatfield were active supporters of the UMWA. Matewan was a non-union camp and not by choice. Miners who lived and worked just north of Mingo and Logan County had experienced the same brutality under the same agency a decade or so before. Paint Creek and Cabin Creek were horrific examples of the brutality this company was capable of doing. The railroads and the coal companies paid the Baldwin-Felts Detective Agency to keep it that way. Cabell and Sid worked to support the persecuted minors and their struggle to organize. The mining interests were quietly trying to bribe their way into the miner's network. They looked for any weak link they could find. They wanted to give agents greater access to the miners' everyday activities, especially clandestine meetings. Meetings attended by Sid and Cabell were the highest priority. There were many such meetings to support the unionization effort in Mingo County. All the while, the atmosphere was like looking at the darkest of clouds before you have to take shelter. Somehow, I can imagine it being like the French Resistance in 1941. Meetings and communications must have been enigmatic. No one knew for sure whose allegiance could be reversed for a bag of cash. Spies were all about.

Baldwin-Felts sent agents into the taverns, the restaurants, and even the mines. They tried to somehow get permission to install fixed machine guns in strategic locations around the perimeter of this very small town. Neither Cabell nor Sid would cooperate with these unconstitutional demands. Think about that. If anyone requested the local government to place machine guns at your welcome center, would you be able to respond? If so, how? This actually happened. This atmosphere led to greater and greater distance between peace and violence. Inescapable brutality was just around the corner. The Summer of 1920 in Matewan was electric. The power and influence of William Balwdin's detective agency versus the collective energy of the people he tried to manipulate must have been explosive. Revolution was in the air. Uprising was discussed in the homes, the taverns, the churches, and wherever Sid and Cabell chose to meet. Workers from completely different cultures were forced to unite toward a singular solution. Their only option was to organize and join the UMWA. Their newfound hope was the skinny police chief. This was his destiny, and there was no way he could walk away from it.

In January 1920, the UMWA staged a massive campaign to organize over 3,000 miners in Southern West Virginia. Because the policies of the mining companies (mostly) disallowed union membership, those 3,000 miners were fired, or dismissed one way or another. For those who rented houses owned by the mining company, they were evicted. Several hundred families were cast out of their homes with no job and nowhere to go. Even if they wanted to leave, there were no roads to take them away from Matewan. Many others refused to vacate. The Balwin-Felts detective agency was tasked with forcible removal of these families. They were widespread among the small villages throughout Southern West Virginia. The mountainous terrain added to the difficulty of this task. It wasn't until May 19th, 1920 that the detectives arrived in Matewan. By then, everyone knew what they were capable of doing, and everyone knew this would be the last straw.

May 19th, 1920, a Wednesday, was a warm and rainy day. Occasional showers fell from intermittent clouds. It was a typical late Spring day in Matewan. About one half of the Baldwin-Felts detectives arrived by train sometime in the morning. Among these agents was Lee Felts. Albert Felts was already in the area scouting out their mission. They didn't bring their Death Special train car--I'll give them that. In all, there were 13 agents dispatched to Matewan. They quickly spread out to their assigned addresses and forcibly removed the remaining miners who refused eviction. Those miners' possessions were thrown out onto the street. The agents were well armed so there wasn't much the miners could do. In many cases, the husband was at work when the detectives knocked on the door. For the most part, the detectives threw out women and children. Sometime in the late afternoon, the wind of these evictions reached the chief of police. Sid Hatfield, along with mayor Cabell Testerman, organized a sizable group of miners (militiamen?) and waited until the agents were ready to depart town. This was about 4 pm. Main street was probably a mud fest by this time. All eyes were fixed on the train station.

The original Matewan train depot; circa 1920. This photo was graciously provided by a lifelong citizen of Mingo County. This building no longer exists today.

As the 13 Baldwin-Felts agents returned to the train station, Sid and his angry mob quickly approached. Albert and Lee would be the spokesmen for the agents. Sid was the voice of Matewan. Sid tried to arrest the agents and Albert and Lee tried to arrest Sid. Sid's argument was that the evictions violated the law. Albert and Lee Felts argued Sid was interfering with a legal action on behalf of the mining company's personal property. Shouting began and the sabers came out. Suddenly, someone fired a shot and all hell broke loose.

Modern day view, parallel to the post office, looking into downtown Matewan. If you visit, you can feel the history. The shootout was mainly along the railroad tracks, one street over.

At the corner of town is the old U.S. post office. It's just upriver from the current train station replica. This building begins the three-block stretch of downtown Matewan. It sits alongside the train tracks.

These buildings were business oriented on the ground level, but the upper floors were mostly residential. In the upper rooms, snipers were patiently awaiting any confrontation. Sid planned this, and the townsfolk were eager to comply. Once the first shot was fired, (probably Sid's assassination of Albert Felts) all the windows swung open. Out came the long guns. A wild west style gun fight erupted, and hundreds of rounds were fired in a one/two-minute melee. When it was over, seven Balwdin-Felts detectives and three townsfolk lay dead in the unpaved streets of Matewan. The UMWA realized its goal of full contact, but this was only a single scene in a very long play. This day was a good day for the union, or so they thought. It was a necessary victory, but it was very barbaric, like almost everything in this era. The celebration of victory was inevitable, and I'm sure it too was barbaric. There would be a great number of hangovers the next morning. The families that the detectives threw out were able gather their possessions and go home. They would sleep comfortably that night. There was no fear of Baldwin-Felts detectives, at least this night.

Among the dead were Albert and Lee Felts. Also killed was Matewan mayor Cabell Testerman. I tried to write my own version of this event, but I was too kind. It was so barbaric, I have trouble with how awful this night must have been. The following is from a framed manuscript in the Matewan Visitors Center. It's way more raw and graphic than any of my research discovered. It may be sensationalized, but it may be true. Here is my synopsis of this document. You can view it for yourself at the Matewan Visitors Center.

1. Sid for sure killed Albert Felts. He shot him point blank in the head. Front or back is in question. I belive it was the front.

2. Lee Felts was killed by Ed Chamber's father, Reece Chambers.

3. It speculates Sid shot his best friend and mayor of Matewan, Ed Chambers. This will never be known for sure, but I suspect he did.

4. It alleges an affair between Sid and Ed's wife, Jessie. Again, no way to prove this. However, they did marry two weeks later.

5. Baldwin-Felts agent C. B. Cunningham was shot 17 times but was somehow still alive. He was "straightened up" to take a final shot to the forehead by Sid. Sid is quoted as saying, "Boy, that GD SOB sure had a heap of guts." This is probably true.

6. Rev. Bob Mullins, a miner, was shot next to the Matewan National Bank. Tot Tinsley was the other resident killed. He was an innocent bystander.

7. E.O. Powell, a Baldwin-Felts agent, was wounded, but survived the initial massacre. His body was found later in an alley (McCoy Alley?) with nine bullet wounds.

8. The 4 pm "Sixteen" train pulled into town just as the smoke was lifting. No passenger disembarked. Witnesses say they saw townsfolk spitting tobacco juice into the eyes of the dead agents. What a sight that must have been.

9. One Baldwin-Felts agent escaped by swimming across the Tug Fork to KY.

10. One agent hid in a cooper's barrel for six hours. It doesn't say this, but it would have been after 10 pm when he emerged and therefore very dark by then. He survived.

11. The Anderson brothers, Baldwin-Felts agents, boarded the traumatized train and posed as passengers. One was wounded, the other was not. They both escaped the massacre.

12. The article does not account for the final surviving agent. It's possible there were only 12 agents, and not 13.

These "trophies" were the main street decorations for the wild celebration that followed into the wee hours of May 20th.. After the party, featuring random shots fired into the dead bodies of the Baldwin-Felts detectives, and many jugs of moonshine, the local coroner was barely able to identify the bodies the following morning. This is the definition of hate. Sid Hatfield emplified this show of force. The result was inevitable.

Old U.S. Post Office in Matewan. There are bullets lodged in the mortar of this building from the massacre. It was in every shooter's crossfire for one, maybe two minutes that day. This was the hornet's nest.

Adjacent to the railroad tracks, this stretch of Main Street in Matewan was booming with business in 1920. Every room in these buildings was filled with residents. Every business was thriving. Every square foot of real estate was occupied. Everyone was connected. Imagine the upper windows opening with high powered rifles firing in the massacre. The muddy streets must have been obscured by the smoke of all that gun fire, at least for a while. Blood was everywhere.

Bullets lodged in the side of the Matewan post office. They appear to be .50 caliper in size.

Historical marker between the old post office and the visitor's center. Lots of history to the left and the right of this marker. (The marker says 12. But Albert Felts was already there.)

The town of Matewan. I'm standing on the very active train tracks by old Main St. The old post office is on the extreme left of this picture but is not included. This is where the massacre happened on May 19th, 1920. The original train depot would have been on the far left.

Sid Hatfield survived the shootout. The vast majority of the miners involved survived as well. It will never be known for sure if Sid killed Albert and/or Lee Felts. I believe he killed at least one of them, but there is no way to prove this. Regardless, Thomas Felts would paint a very large bullseye on Sid Hatfield. Both of his brothers were suddenly dead. Good guy or bad guy, that's a pretty strong motivator for action. Thomas had the luxury of time to plan his revenge, which he would happily do. Thomas Felts was an academic and very much a thinker. He has no history of rash decisions, at least any I can find. Yet, it's not hard to guess his target. I can only imagine what esoteric and cryptic revenges he must have planned. Mr. Charles E. Lively was likely involved with these conversations.

Miles to Go

As the dust settled from the battle, Sid would marry Cabell Testerman's widow within two weeks of his death. They were married in Huntington, WV on June 2nd, 1920. They spent their second night in Huntington in the city jail on 4th Ave. and 7th St. Upon their arrival to Huntington, the first night, they were officially un-married. They stayed in a local hotel and were arrested for "improper relations" by the Huntington Police Dept. I wonder who knew this, and who notified the police. He was quite the celebrity by now, and there were certainly many forces aligned against him. They had their marriage license, all their papers and such, but they had yet to have the ceremony. Once released from jail the next day, they promptly tied the knot. I can't say where, but I believe it was in the Cabell County WV courthouse. I also couldn't find any details about their honeymoon, but Huntington was a thriving and bustling city in 1920. There were tall buildings, a streetcar system, and thriving factories. There were many restaurants and merchants to choose from. Shopping options were international. Anything you could want was just a tram car away. The city was vibrant and wealthy, mostly from the coal that was produced about 100 miles away.

Purchased in 1908, the city maintains a park that sits on the South-Side of Huntington. Known as Ritter Park, it would have been a short streetcar ride from downtown. Although there is no known documentation of Sid & Jessie making a visit here, I believe they did. It is a premier destination in Huntington and quite a beautiful place. It would have been beautiful in 1920 as well.

Ritter Park in Huntington, WV. It's a serene place with several miles of walking paths and other attractions. I imagine Sid and Jessie took a stroll along these trails.

Established in 1902 as a picnic area by the Camden Interstate Railway, there was a significant amusement destination called Camden Park in the West End of Huntington. It featured a carousel, roller coasters and numerous other rides. It was anything but Matewan. If Sid and Jessie went there, I'm certain they had fun. But I'm sure reality rebounded quickly as they soon returned to Matewan. The massacre was the beginning of a very active shooting war between the UMWA interests and the mining companies. More violence was just beyond the horizon. The apex of violence was like the roller coaster reaching the summit of elevation. The thrill was palpable, but you knew it would be a terrifying ride downhill. The honeymoon was over. It was back to work. No more cotton candy or snow cones any time soon.

When Sid arrived back in Matewan, he was quite the celebrity. He had provided the miners with a significant glimpse of justice. It was bloody because the conditions leading up to this event were so barbaric to begin with. There was a brief window to celebrate a pause in the Baldwin-Felts reign of terror. The miners were energized by their new and undisputed leader. With the support of the UMWA, Sid Hatfield starred in a short film reenacting the deadly confrontation in Matewan. The union used this film to harvest support from the more tepid miners who were reluctant to join. Momentum had swung toward the union and away from the fear of the Baldwin-Felts detectives. But it was a short lived respite from a long term conflict. Thomas Felts was on the war path, and Sid was his number one target. He would use his legal training and detective instincts to find a way to rid the miners of Sid and thus any hope of justice.

For the remainder of the Summer of 1920, Sid Hatfield maintained his position as chief of police of Matewan. When his term expired, he ran for (and won) the position of Constable of Magnolia. There were no other major shoot-outs or massacres, but there were strikes, skirmishes, and much agitation on behalf of both sides of the conflict. The UMWA moved about with more freedom and continued to organize miners.

With both Albert and Lee Felts dead, the Baldwin-Felts agency lost a significant chunk of leadership. But Thomas Felts was anything but done. He was busy fabricating legal charges against Sid and a host of miners involved in the massacre. He would finally get a charge to stick late in 1920. The charge would be for the murder of his brother, Albert Felts. I find this interesting because it implies that Sid Hatfield did indeed kill Albert. The trial would take place in the Mingo Co. town of Williamson. This is the county seat of government and the largest town in Mingo County, then and today. It would ultimately be yet another defeat for Thomas Felts.

The Coal House in downtown Williamson. This magnificent building is made entirely of coal. Well worth a visit. The building on the left is the current courthouse and jail. Built in 1969, this is not the jail where Sid was held. That jail no longer exists.

Williamson is about 20 miles downriver from Matewan. Interestingly, that makes it 20 miles north of Matewan. It was (and still is) the largest town in Mingo County. Prior to the trial's opening statements on January 28, 1921, the Baldwin-Felts detective agency placed about 40 armed detectives along the streets of Williamson to intimidate the perceived bias of the jury. The local citizens of Williamson were not indifferent to the struggles of their neighbors in Matewan. They faced the same persecution as Matewan, but to a lesser degree. Thomas Felts believed any jury selected in this county would be sympathetic to the UMWA and therefore Sid Hatfield. Like I said, he was a pretty smart dude. It was a cold day with blustery winds from the northwest. The Baldwin-Felts guards must have been bundled up tight.

Thomas's premonition was correct, and his tactic of intimidation was ineffective. In fact, it was probably counterproductive. Sid Hatfield was acquitted along with 19 co-defendants. I can see Sid Hatfield walking out of the courthouse after the longest murder trial (to date) in West Virginia's history. I imagine him flashing his gold-plated teeth at the freezing Baldwin-Felts detectives as he walked off the commons a free man. I bet Thomas Felts almost had an aneurysm after learning about the verdict. I further believe Mr. Felts decided that his next move against Sid Hatfield would be anything but legal. It just needed to be effective. After this trial fiasco, I believe he chose to go nuclear. The only question was ... how to do it?

The Impetus for Blair Mountain

By the year 1919, almost all of the Appalachian coal fields were unionized. The exceptions were Logan and Mingo counties in southwestern part of the state. A combination of the coal operators, the local sheriffs, and the Baldwin-Felts detective agency remained effective in preventing the UMWA from any reasonable representation of the miners. After the Matewan massacre of May 1920, the UMWA District 17, placed a large bullseye on this region. But, these two counties were a fortress to the UMWA.

One of the other values that placed stress on the miners was the post WW1 recession. Whereas the union miners in other parts of the state were able to maintain their wage base and representation, the non-union miners in Logan and Mingo counties were forced to accept lower wages and/or termination if they didn't completely commit to the desire of their employer. On July 1st, 1920, these wage practices caused another strike by the miners in these two counties. There would be many strikes in 1920 and 1921. Even though a majority of the miners in these two counties were now union members, they were not able to receive complete support from the UMWA. They could join the union, but the union could do very little to help them secure their employment, let alone their wages. It was a stalemate that went on for over 30 years in Mingo and Logan counties. You could join the union, but to what effect?

During the time between the Matewan Massacre and the other events that caused the Blair Mountain event, Sid Hatfield was very active in disrupting the mining company interests. But, as an officer of the law, I question how much physical involvement he had. I think his rockstar influence was more than enough to incite others to do his wishes. He was quite famous by this time. His followers were very loyal to him, and some of them were prone to violence. Sometime after his acquittal of the Matewan Massacre in March 1921, and later into May 1921, he was supposedly involved in a dynamite attack against a coal tipple in Mohawk, WV, in neighboring McDowell County. Whether or not he actually participated, or simply coordinated the attack, is questionable to me. The attack happened, but the responsible party will likely remain hidden forever. It is quite possible Thomas Felts paid local roughians to carry out this attack. But as the smoldering ashes of the coal tipple faded away, McDowell County prepared an indictment for Sid Hatfield. This much is certain.

The majority of the mines were open, but many of the miners were forced to sign "yellow dog" contracts that were drafted by the mining companies. Basically, their employment was contingent on them remaining out of the union. These contracts were declared legal by the Supreme Court's Adair v. United States decision in 1908. On the other hand, the union miners were furious, and they engaged in numerous acts of violence and sabotage against the non-union mines. Part of the reason was the non-union miners were paid less than the union miners, and this lowered the prevailing wage base. Martial law was declared three times by the governor of West Virginia during this time frame. Both sides were violent. Both sides were equitable in their potential for savagery.

For weeks on end, there was gunfire all along the Tug Fork River basin. From just South of Williamson to just South of Matewan, high powered rifles would trade shots across the Tug Fork river just after sunset and throughout the night. The citizens could not know when the shooting would start, and they could not know when it would stop.

A lifelong citizen of Matewan told me her grandparents were well practiced in blowing out every lamp quickly. She told me when the shooting began, you got as low as you could, double time. If your home had a cellar, or basement, you would go there. If not, you would go behind your home and stay as low to the ground as possible for as long as you had to. Can you imagine? Living in Mingo County, in 1920, was quite dangerous. She told me the miners on the WV side were supporters of the UMWA. The miners on the KY side were "scabs" for the most part. It seems like there were many tribes fighting each other. I believe the only tribe that was truly organized was the Baldwin-Felts Detective Agency, at least at this moment. That would account for a lot of unfocused energy, which would perpetuate the unrest of the time. How unfortunate.

The weapons the miners used varied anywhere from black powder muzzle loaded rifles to calipers and loads we enjoy today. Kill zones were easily a mile away. Because many of the locals had been soldiers in WWI, they were intimately knowledgeable of the most effective weapons available at the time. The most likely rifles they possessed were either the British Enfield .303 or the German Mauser 7.92 mm. Either of these two weapons could effectively kill a man at a half mile distance. The Winchester 30-30 was also prevalent, as well as the French made 8 mm 1886 Lepel rifle. All of these deadly weapons, and many more, were in common use in 1920. The Mauser claimed the greatest kill range of just over 4,000 yards. All of them had a muzzle velocity of over 2,000 fps. The gun technology of 1921 far exceeded the gun technologies of the previous century. These were very lethal weapons that were well ahead of their time. The people living along the Tug knew this very well. They took this technology very seriously. They had to patch bullet holes in their homes on a regular basis.

If a miner decided to engage in this tit-for-tat warfare, he would need to find higher ground. There would also need to be some sort of natural cover. Many rock formations jutted out of the mountains. There were old logging roads, as well. Once you found your spot, you needed some basic provisions to sustain your position. Water, some basic food, and tobacco were essential. However, you could not produce any light or fire so you couldn't smoke a cigarette. If you did smoke, you would compromise your position by giving off even the slightest gleam of light. And so, there became an alternative to smoking cigarettes. The Wheeling, West Virginia based Bloch

Brothers Tobacco Co., AKA The Helme Tobacco Co., produced Mail Pouch chewing tobacco.

They were originally a cigar manufacturer founded in 1879. They realized (like all the other cigar manufacturers) they could collect the unused cigar clippings and add sweeteners, usually molasses, and flavors to create a new product. Chewing tobacco and snuff were very common among these fighters. They could enjoy their tobacco without getting shot at unnecessarily. The snipers dotted along both sides of the Tug Fork and would trade shots while spitting tobacco juice on the native daffodils and daisies. This form of tobacco also allowed the use of both hands since one hand wasn't occupied with a cigarette. It was gross, but nonetheless logical.

Eventually, the shooters would run out of ammunition, or simply get hungry and tired. The beleaguered fighters could finally crawl back to their bedrooms and sleep through what was left of the night. This event went on for over a year.

The first incident was known as the "Three Day War." This happened in June of 1920. It is estimated over 200,000 rounds of ammunition were fired during these three days. (H.B. Lee "Bloodletting in Appalachia" Pages 73-74) The next event was in March 1921. The latter event was even more violent than the first one. Newly elected WV governor E. F. Morgan declared martial law and sent in Major Tom B Davis to quell the insurrection. This was about the same time Sid Hatfield was acquitted in Williamson. It is not known how many people died during this war within a war. Both sides carried their dead to places unknown. Neither side reported their casualties because there was no one with whom to report them.

Thomas Zeroes In

On July 14th, 1921, Sid Hatfield found out he was the target of a conspiracy charge related to the attack on the coal tipple in Mohawk, WV. This property is located in neighboring McDowell County, near the headwaters of the Tug Fork. It's only about one mile from the Mingo County line. In about a fortnight, he would travel back to McDowell county to face yet another trial. It would be his last trial.

Throughout the tumultuous year of 1921 in Mingo County, Sid Hatfield was under constant legal assault. I believe some of the charges against him may have been warranted. I think most were not. Either way, it was an all-out war between the pro-union and anti-union forces. Real people died and real justice was subjective at best. In many cases, innocent people were charged with crimes, and criminals were allowed to go free. Some things never change. I believe Thomas Felts was pulling many strings, behind the scenes, to find a more favorable setting with which to lure Sid Hatfield into his plan. In this scenario, Sid would have no concept of a set-up. Thomas' instincts led him to believe Sid would show up for any legal proceeding no matter what. He had beaten them all thus far, so what's another bogus trial anyway? Sid probably believed this was just another trial that he would walk away from. I believe Thomas finally found his moment of opportunity with the trial in McDowell County, West Virginia. The date was August 1st, 1921. The place was Welch, West Virginia, county seat of McDowell County, in extreme Southern West Virginia.

McDowell County courthouse in Welch, WV. It was constructed in 1893 by architect Frank P. Milburn and was added to the National Register of Historic Places in August 1979. Sid Hatfield was murdered at the top of these steps in August 1921.

Charles Everett Lively was the quintessential spy in the West Virginia mine wars. His allegiance fell firmly on the doorstep of the Baldwin-Felts detective agency, but he was very clever at concealing his fidelity to Bill and Tom. He was about the same age as Sid and maybe a bit taller. He was, I think, more polished than Sid, but only because he was comfortable mingling among the detectives and politicians of society. Maybe he was even more daring than Sid. He slithered between the commanders of two, warring factions and befriended both. To me, that would test about anyone's nerves. He became a dues-paying member of the United Mine Workers of America, District 17, sometime before WW1. But soon after, he reported conversations, hearsay, and comments to Thomas Felts, probably directly. He was hand-picked. He was the "boots on the ground" for the agency. He was quite adept at playing both sides of a conflict. He was smooth in his demeanor, even likable, but also very capable of killing. He must have been promised a sizable bag of cash by Baldwin-Felts to so completely deceive the leadership of the UMWA, and especially Sid.

He must have been a very intelligent man to be such an effective double agent. He was never held accountable for his unreported crimes. His betrayal and murder of Sid Hatfield should be legend. But, it's not. He also betrayed the UMWA significantly, and for a very long time.

He was born March 6th, 1887 in Davis Creek, WV, just south of the capital of Charleston. He died in Huntington, WV at the age of 75 on May 28th, 1962. In 1902, he became a coal miner at the age of 14. He was an early member of the UMWA. Exactly when he joined the Baldwin-Felts agency is unknown. C.E. Lively moved around the state taking mining jobs at various locations. He was even a delegate for the UMWA conventions and served as Vice President of a UMWA local. All the while, he was feeding intelligence to the Baldwin-Felts detective agency. In the Summer of 1920, just after the Matewan Massacre, he was assigned to Matewan as a result of the UMWA's massive campaign drive there. Prior to that, he worked at their headquarters in Charleston. Shortly after arriving in Matewan, he was hired as a miner in a local coal mine. (That must have been a hard transition.) Ultimately, he lost his job for inappropriate conduct with union supporters. (Honestly, I have no idea what that means.)

After he lost his job, he opened a popular restaurant in Matewan. I wonder where a poor miner, who was recently fired, was able to raise the capital for such a significant investment? His restaurant, located in the same building the miners used to meet for union discussions, was in the downstairs part of the building. This was, more or less, the unofficial union hall. It was in this restaurant he befriended Sid. He was well liked by the pro-union populace. He smiled with them and served them delightful food, and he agreed with their grievances. All the while, he was preparing his next telegraph to Thomas Felts.

During the January 1921 Matewan Massacre trial of Sid and 19 other defendants for the murder of Albert Felts, Charles E Lively revealed his true identity and testified against Sid Hatfield. I believe he was compelled to do so by Thomas Felts. I think Thomas had too much confidence that this jury would convict Sid Hatfield. He committed his most valuable intel asset. He unmasked Charles Lively and it didn't work. Thomas Felts pushed all the legal weight he had to remove Sid. He either wins big or loses big. After the acquittal, Charles was not seen in Matewan again. He would meet Sid only once more after the trial in Williamson. He would still be on the payroll of Thomas Felts.

The Road to Welch

Mohawk, WV is in McDowell County. It's less than one mile from the Mingo County line. There's not much there, then or today. The local coal tipple was "shot up" and dynamite was used in one form or another during an attack. The tipple was almost completely destroyed. Witnesses (probably people paid by Baldwin-Felts) placed Sid Hatfield and Ed Chambers at the scene, but I don't think they were there, and I don't think they did it. That said, their indictment would be in McDowell County. In late July 1921, Sid and Ed boarded a train in Matewan, with their wives, and left for the county seat of McDowell County. The trial date was set for August 1st, 1921.

Sid and Ed arrived in Welch with assurances from McDowell County sheriff Bill Hatfield that they would be fully protected. But the sheriff left town the day before their arrival. He went to Craig Healing Springs, VA for some personal time off. I believe he was told to leave by Thomas Felts or one of his agents. Whether or not this is true, the fact is he left town on July 31st, and therefore could not offer the promised protection.

Sid and Ed hired attorney C. J. Van Fleet from Pittsburgh as their counsel. He specialized in union representation. Upon their arrival to Welch, Mr. Van Fleet went to a local hotel to reserve a room for both families. Sid, Ed and their wives were soon checked in. Upon advice from counsel, they left their firearms in the hotel room. I can't prove it, but Sid probably brought his SW .44 pistol to Welch. After accommodations were squared, they planned a stroll to the courthouse. Just as they were leaving, there was an unexpected long-distance phone call for attorney Van Fleet. He had to take the call, so Sid, Ed, and their wives traveled on to the courthouse without their attorney and without their guns. This phone call may have saved Mr. Van Fleet's life. On the other hand, maybe not. These circumstances seem very convenient to me. No weapon, no lawyer, and no clue. The weather was warm with no rain. It was partly cloudy with high humidity. Still, it would have been a rather pleasant walk from the hotel to the courthouse.

Modern day Welch, WV. This vantage point is on the County courthouse steps. This is likely where Sid first saw the face of Charles Lively, standing with three others on the courthouse lawn, a half flight more away. He could go back down and forever be a coward, or he could continue to the top of the stairs. He continued up the stairs. He didn't have a weapon. The four agents had weapons.

Just like the Baldwin-Felts detectives in the Matewan Massacre a little over a year earlier, Sid and Ed had no idea what was about to happen. They were completely ambushed. They were unarmed in a foreign town, and probably unconcerned because they had won every battle thus far. As you can see in the pictures, the steps to the McDowell County courthouse have an approach from both directions of the

Welch, WV view from the common landing of the courthouse steps. I believe Charles Lively was standing very close to here.

city sidewalk. They combine into one flight midway up the incline. As Sid Hatfield and Ed Chambers began the ascent to the courthouse commons, they noticed an assembly of several men. They were ominous looking men. Among them was Charles E. Lively, George "Buster" Pence, and William Salters. I imagine Sid's heart skipped a beat when he recognized the face of his one-time friend, Charles Lively, standing on the courthouse commons. I'm sure he was immediately reminded he left his weapon in the hotel room. I'm guessing it was the Smith & Wesson .44 magnum. His lawyer gave him bad advice for this place and time. Was that planned? We'll never know for sure. At this point, there was no other move than to continue upstairs. If he turned and ran, he would be a coward—which is something he was never accused of being. If he continued up the steps, he was dead. I believe he knew this. The two men and their wives continued to the top of the stairway and on to the common grounds of the McDowell County Courthouse. I believe Sid knew exactly what was about to happen. When he reached the top of the stairs, he threw his hands up, smiled with his gold-plated teeth and said, "Hello boys!"

The Murder of Sid

As soon as they took the last step to the courthouse, a hail of bullets exploded from this band of Baldwin-Felts employees. Sid was hit with three shots to the chest and one more to his torso. He died almost instantly. Ed was shot three times and fell down the steps to the first landing. His wife ran to his aid and hovered over his still-breathing body. Charles Lively walked down the second flight of steps and fired the final shot into the head of Ed Chambers. Meanwhile, the fourth detective, Hughey Lucas, fired all six rounds from his revolver into the limestone face of the courthouse. The group formed a cordon around the event to keep spectators from witnessing the scene. Smoke was thick from all the bullets fired. As it slowly lifted, Sid Hatfield had an empty revolver in his hand. It would remain that way until the police arrived. It wasn't Sid's gun, but that's how it was done. George "Buster" Pence was well known for saying, "Kill 'em with one gun, and hand 'em another." I'm pretty sure this is exactly what happened. (H.B. Lee. Bloodletting in Appalachia.)

Neither of the wives were injured. Jessie Testerman, now Jessie Hatfield, was a widow twice inside 14 months. Her love affair and life's adventure came to a crashing halt on August 1st, 1921. I cannot imagine her pain. With what they went through, in the smallest of time, I have no doubt he was madly in love with her, and she loved him as much, or maybe more. But I sometimes wonder ... Was she that attracted to Sid, to re-marry inside of two weeks, or was she simply wise to choose a man who offered the greatest chance of survival? Maybe, it was both. It was a super-harsh time that most people wouldn't understand. Regardless, her ultimate justice is the tipping point in the life of the Baldwin-Felts detective agency.

They could not have known, but this event marked the pinnacle of the Baldwin-Felts influence in Appalachia. Nothing changed overnight, but the winds of justice were beginning to swell. Baldwin-Felts would grow no higher. The beginning of their end happened on the courthouse steps in Welch that day. The gathering clouds of the next conflict were about to drench everyone. It would be even more bloody than anything they had experienced before. Thomas Felts had about one week to gloat and smile. However, he could not have planned on what would happen next. I don't think anyone could.

State historical marker at the McDowell County courthouse in Welch, WV.

Charles Everett Lively, George Pence, and William Salter were indicted for the murder of Sid and Ed in McDowell County. However, William Baldwin and Thomas Felts knew exactly what would happen regarding the verdict of the murder of Sid. That's why they planned this whole affair. McDowell County was completely controlled by the coal companies and the detectives they paid to do their work. I hate to admit it, but it was brilliant planning. At the subsequent murder trial for these defendants, all the jury members were either fearful for their lives or were paid by the mining interests (probably both). All defendants were acquitted on the premise of self-defense, as was normal in this place and time. William and Thomas had finally rid themselves of Sid Hatfield. However, they opened a whole new can of worms that I seriously doubt they considered. This was their only flaw in an otherwise very well constructed plan. They didn't consider the human reaction.

The only true hero the miners ever knew was suddenly gone. The only guy that actually did something was viciously murdered. The vacuum of hope would need to be replaced by something big, and quickly. Absolute rage was the only flag flying for the common miner. The state government couldn't or wouldn't help. Martial Law only inflamed the situation. The union couldn't do much either. The miners had been on their own for so long that just about anyone who stood up to the injustice would be a hero. And suddenly, they had no hero. Thus began the largest civil insurrection in American history. It would happen in neighboring Logan County. It would begin a little over three weeks from Sid's death. It is known as the Battle of Blair Mountain.

⤳ Blair Mountain ⤳

Historical marker at Blair, WV. Located along WV St. Rte 17, it's a rough ride from Stollings, WV.

To understand this next chapter, you first have to understand Logan County Sheriff, Don Chafin. Whereas Mingo County was dominated by the mining companies, the railroad companies (the Baldwin-Felts detectives and others), Logan County was dominated by a single man. He was no less than a czar. During his reign, if you wanted to be a public-school teacher in Logan County, you would need the approval of Don. If that didn't happen, then "you" didn't happen. No organization, or any political structure existed that could challenge his rule inside the boundaries of Logan County, WV. He was the sunrise and sunset for every citizen. He had armed guards posted at every entry point into the county, which, at the time, was basically limited to railways only. If you were trying to enter Logan County, between 1912 and 1924, you had to have approval from Don Chafin, one way or another. He ran an island nation for many years. His greatest victory was the battle of Blair Mountain, starting in late August 1921. It was less than a month after the murder of Sid Hatfield. He didn't deserve this victory, in my opinion, but he won it nonetheless.

Don Chafin would ride the Blair Mountain fame to his death in a 12th story penthouse, in Huntington, WV on August 9th, 1954. He was a West Virginia Delegate in the 1924 Democratic National Convention. He spent two years in federal prison for violating prohibition, the 18th Amendment to the Constitution. He got busted for moonshine distribution. He attended Marshall College, in Huntington, WV for two years, though he did not receive any degree. He was shot in the chest more than once.

One of those two men that shot him, in an office in Charleston, WV, was Bill Petrey. This event happened in Charleston in September 1919. It was in the UMWA Headquarters. Bill Petrey was the vice-president of UMWA District 17. Sheriff Chafin was in town, drunk, and looking for a fight. As usual, he was also armed. He claimed to have a warrant for the arrest of a union employee. But the warrant was issued in Logan County. For reasons that defy logic, he barged into the office of Bill Petrey and a heated argument ensued. Chafin had no jurisdiction in Kanawha County, but nonetheless demanded Petrey turn over the employee for arrest. Bill Petrey, threatened with serious harm from a drunk Sheriff Chafin, pulled a .22 caliber pistol from his top desk drawer and shot him in the chest. Chafin would survive the shooting. Petrey later remarked, "That's what happens when a man carries a toy pistol. That GD SOB is liable to get well. I should have had my old 44." (H.B. Lee. Bloodletting in Appalachia)

During the battle of Blair Mountain, Chafin rented three biplane aircraft from outside sources to record aerial reconnaissance of the miners' march to Logan. He recruited local citizens (civilians) to volunteer in an armed conflict. He requested, and received, federal troops to assist in defending the city of Logan, WV. But more than anything else, he received a lot of money from the coal companies and to a lesser extent, the railroad companies, to suppress union formation in Logan County. (I can't prove this.) Whereas the Baldwin-Felts detectives in Mingo County carried out the wishes of William Baldwin and Thomas Felts, Don Chafin reigned in another world, if only the next county north. If Sheriff Don needed help, he would hire agents from the Baldwin-Felts detective agency, or someone else. So, in Logan County, William & Tom were the employees, but only if need be. In 1921, there was only room for one emperor. The Czar of Logan was Sheriff Don. Baldwin-Felts only played a supporting role here. Don Chafin wanted a fight. Bill and Tom were happy to assist. To them, it was just another job in an industry they were very good at doing.

The battle of Blair Mountain is very well documented. It was the first time our government dropped bombs (or at least tried to) from airplanes on United States citizens. Excluding the Civil War, this battle involved more Federal troops to quell an insurrection than any other to date. Yet, President Harding did not invoke the Insurrection Act of 1807. Interestingly, George H. W. Bush used this Act in 1992 during the Los Angeles rioting from the Rodney King incident, which was the last time this act was invoked. President Harding could have easily invoked this act, but he did not.

The battle of Blair Mountain occurred from late August into early September 1921. Don Chafin was the unofficial "general" of the non-union forces that would successfully repel an invasion of armed miners into his county. During this battle, President William Harding dispatched 2,000 army regulars to the region to support Don Chafin and his deputies. Over three million rounds of ammunition were fired during this five-day conflict. Archeologists and history buffs are still finding artifacts on this mountain. This battle was Don Chafin's finest moment in his stormy life. For a guy that was so wrong, he planned this battle well, and he won. He set the union back for over 10 years. Here is how it happened . . .

Clouds Gather

Before I get into the details of this incredible event, there first needs to be some context. The year was 1921. The place was (mostly) Logan County, WV, but also Boone County, WV. This was the pinnacle of violence during all the years of the WV Mine Wars. It was 100 years ago. After the murder of Sid Hatfield, whatever semblance of a civil society that remained was now completely gone.

On August 7th, 1921, just one week after Sid's passing, the president of UMWA District 17, Frank Keeney, called for all union miners to assemble on the Capitol grounds in Charleston, WV. It was a warm afternoon with no rain. It is estimated over 5,000 miners were in attendance. This event was the headwaters of the battle of Blair Mountain. It would quickly grow in size and vigor from that meeting. The murder of Sid Hatfield ignited the masses. The Italians, the African Americans, the Irish, the Slavs, the Scots, the Germans, the Poles, and every other national origin that lived there found themselves on the WV State Capitol grounds for a grand event that promised compelling speakers. It was quite the festival. It was peaceful, but it was deadly serious.

There was a surprise speaker planned for this event. None other than Mother Jones took the stage to whip the miners into hysteria. Her foul language and casual indiscretion with the truth was both expected and effective. She cited multiple atrocities committed by the mine operators against the miners. Most incidents were simply made-up, but there's no doubting similar events really did happen. The miners believed her. In one way or another, they had all seen or felt her examples. The truth didn't matter in this speech. They needed something to believe. Once she finished her speech, she gave the chair back to Frank Keeney. Frank waited until the crowd settled into a reasonable quiet. He explained that he had asked Governor E. F. Morgan to lift martial law in Mingo County, but Morgan refused. And so, Frank made the following plea to the assembled miners:

> "Therefore, you have no recourse except to fight. The only way you can get your rights is with a high-power rifle, and the man who does not have this equipment is not a good union man."
>
> Quote from Howard B. Lee. Bloodletting in Appalachia)

Sitting beside Sid Hatfield, front row, second from the left, is Mother Jones. This picture was provided by a lifelong citizen of Matewan. It was most likely taken in Matewan, sometime in 1921.

A thunderous uproar erupted from this statement. It lasted for quite a while. He allowed the crowd to once again quiet down. The final thoughts of this event were boiled down into two words.

Once the crowd was quieted to a reasonable level, he concluded the rally by saying, "Get ready!"

A week and change after this rally, direction was sent to the miners to meet just south of the West Virginial capitol of Charleston. The GPS was the mouth of Lens Creek, in Marmet, WV. This quiet hamlet sits on the banks of the Kanawha River. It was part of the salt mining region of Kanawha County dating back to the early 19th century. It was a direct stop on the old James River Turnpike. It's a very old town. Everyone knew exactly where this destination was located.

Like many streams and rivers in this region, Lens Creek flows north. So, if you marched upstream, you would be marching south, more or less. On August 24th, 1921, approximately 6,000 miners were well provisioned, armed, and ready to march to Logan. Virtually every weapon in the surrounding counties had been purchased, borrowed, or loaned to this newly formed army. (In West Virginia, that would have been a lot of guns, then and now.)

Lawrence "Old Peg-Leg" Dwyer of Beckley, West Virginia, was a member of the International Executive Board of the UMWA. He provided the miners with a fully operational machine gun and 3,000 rounds of ammunition. This gun was stolen from the Baldwin-Felts guards at Willis Branch, WV, (another labor disaster) about a year earlier. That evening, the miners began their 65-mile march to Logan. I can only imagine the spirit and camaraderie shared among these beleaguered miners as they all cheered together. Something was finally being done. They had a machine gun. They had to march in formation and maintain a cadence of steps. They would march through the night, up to and through the headwaters of Lens Creek, then over the next pass. The sun would rise, and they would march on. This is very rugged terrain. What a sight that must have been, so many thousands of men marching through the narrow valleys of Kanawha, Boone, and Logan counties. Marching through this terrain was only conceivable because something was finally happening. And so it went, until they reached the base of Blair Mountain. It's a small patch of flat land in a mountain wilderness. It was barely enough space to accommodate such a great amount of people. This small patch of earth is known as Sharples, West Virginia.

Lens Creek near Marmet in Kanawha County, WV. Hwy 94 follows this stream to its headwaters, and then onto Racine, WV in Boone County. Racine is located on the Little Coal River. From there, the miners followed modern day Rt. 3 to Danville, WV, which is approximately 20 miles from the mouth of Lens Creek. This is a rough ride today. It was rougher in 1921.

Located on US Route 17, along the Spruce Fork stream, Sharples, WV sits on the North base of Blair Mountain. There is enough flat land to accommodate a very large encampment. Otherwise, there's not much there, then or today.

∽ In the Meantime ∽

The governor of West Virginia asked President Harding to send federal troops to intervene in this insurrection. I'm convinced it was also because of a request from Sheriff Don Chafin. Harding issued a proclamation that basically said the miners' march was unlawful. He dispatched General Harry H. Bandholtz to enforce his decree. The Major General served in WW1 and also in the Philippines during the Spanish-American War. The governor and General Bandholtz called Frank Keeney to a meeting and explained that the situation was unlawful and urged compliance with the president's order. If not, the consequence would include the marchers being forcibly disbanded, and the union leaders would be charged with treason. (This issue comes up later.) The general and Mr. Keeney met up with the miners, en route to Logan, and appealed to the leadership to disband. Faced with the consequences, the miners began to pack-up and return to Kanawha County. Was it fear of consequence or fear of failure? In either case, Sid's death was suddenly less of a flash point. Powerful figures had just issued powerful consequences if the march to hang Don Chafin continued. More than 6,000 armed miners must have been totally deflated. A decorated United States general just explained to this rabble that their march was unjust. If they continued, they would be defeated by the United States government, one way or another.

General Bandholtz was satisfied with the meeting and promptly departed for Washington, D.C., the next day. However, he did something really stupid just before his last day in West Virginia. The miners learned that the General (so they were told) had directed a strong dispatch of state troopers and mine guards to move north of Blair Mountain the day before. (I seriously doubt he gave this order.) This detachment of law enforcement moved into union territory and attacked the lead elements of the marching miners—just as they were retreating. They shot and killed two miners, wounded three others, and then quickly retreated back to the city of Logan. This action can only be explained by the absolute hatred between the opposing sides. The conflict was resolved, and the miners were ready to retreat. Why would an unprovoked attack happen and miners killed?

Maybe, Don Chafin directed this detachment to provoke the miners into changing their minds. (This is what I believe.) Regardless, the troopers claimed they were attacked first, and thus their actions were self-defense. This doesn't make sense. Chafin's guards were in enemy territory at the time of the attack. How can you be "attacked" when you cross into your enemy's lines? Again, it was always self-defense. Word of this attack spread like wildfire among the miners. The march to Logan would resume, and very quickly. Only now, there was zero doubt about the possibility of a fight. Don Chafin got his way yet again. He was, afterall, the czar of Logan County. He wanted this fight, and he got his way.

The Original Redneck

On or about August 25th, 1921, Bill Blizzard issued a password to his newly formed army of miners. The password was "To Mingo." Hundreds of the miners were former soldiers from WW1. They understood the seriousness of the situation and expected some model of discipline and direction from their leadership. Because there were no military uniforms among the thousands of miners, and many of the mine guards were not uniformed. Bill directed his army to wear a red bandana around their neck. Virtually every coal miner owned this necessity in 1921. Thus, the legend of the "red neck" was born in Boone County, West Virginia in 1921. General Blizzard sent out reconnaissance to all roads and any possible path or flank to his army. For a very young man with no military experience, he exceeded a lot of expectations. In total, he commanded approximately 6,000 miners. (Some estimates exceed 10,000, but I doubt it was that many.) Their stated goal was to march into Logan, capture sheriff Don Chafin, and hang him in the courthouse square (for real). Then, they would continue to Mingo County, overthrow martial law, and organize the miners in both Logan and Mingo counties. Vengeance, destruction, and actual death were planned by the miners. If planned right, they would also enlist countless new members into the UMWA. "To Mingo" was a go.

All the while, Don Chafin was busy recruiting a strong defense from any resource available in the town of Logan, and elsewhere. He was well aware of the impending battle, but this is what history won't tell you. Don Chafin desperately wanted a fight. He knew he could win it. He was that confident. He was an all-powerful judge and jury, because anyone who challenged him was prone to disappearance. He knew this moment in history was his, and he knew it would make him rich. He was plugged into the political machine of the day. The mining companies simply had more cash, and Don understood how to get paid. I'll give him that.

Whereas Bill Blizzard recruited able-bodied miners for his army, which were plentiful, Don Chafin paid the Baldwin-Felts detective agency to send in reinforcements, and it was more than a few. These men were professionals and they didn't come cheap. Many were ex-military. I'm not sure how he got this invoice through accounts payable, but I'm sure he did. He even went to the Logan city jail and spoke to all the inmates incarcerated there. He summoned them to a common ground and made an offer. Most of them were jailed on bogus charges related to union organization, yet some of them were simply drunks, and some of them were just losers, like anywhere or anytime. His deal was that if they agreed to take up arms against the impending invasion, he would commute their sentences. A handful did, but the vast majority told him to suck it.

One of those inmates was Floyd Greggs, a former U.S. Marine. Mr. Greggs had just arrived in Logan a few days before this commotion and was simply looking for work. He had no idea what was going on. Chafin's goons arrested him soon after he arrived on suspicion of being a union organizer. He was probably roughed up, but he was most certainly thrown into the city jail. Logan had a formidable jail in 1920. It still does, but the original Jail is long since gone.

A few days later, he was escorted to Don Chafin's office in the Logan County courthouse and told to wait for his meeting with the sheriff. When Don Chafin finally arrived for the meeting, he promptly showed Mr. Greggs a wide array of weapons (in his state-owned office) and told him to select the rifle of his choice. Then, he would join Don Chafin's army. This was typical of Don. It was a "take it or leave it" offer. When Greggs refused to pick a weapon, Don did something unimaginable today. According to Howard B Lee, in his book "Bloodletting in Appalachia," Don Chafin put the muzzle of a revolver in Floyd Greggs' face and said, "You will either fight or die." That was Don Chafin's deal. Like almost all of the other inmates, Floyd refused to choose a rifle.

Floyd Greggs had balls. And just like all the rest, he was returned to his cell. Such was the character of Logan County Sheriff Don Chafin. Fortunately for Don, he didn't need the prisoners anyway. Bully for him.

"General" Bill Blizzard, far left, Fred Mooney, Frank Keeney and Bill Petrey. 1921. This photo is from a store front window on Mate St. in Matewan, WV. Bill Blizzard was in his early 20's at the time of this photo. You can view this storefront window today.

By this time, late August into early September 1921, the opposing forces were on an unstoppable collision course. The miners, originally torn between continuing and retreating, had no reservations now. Don Chafin continued to give them every reason to march on. Meanwhile, the Sheriff was scrambling to assemble every ally possible to repel the approaching army. He petitioned the federal government (along with the Governor of West Virginia) to dispatch 2,000 federal troops to support him. This is in addition to the paid forces of Baldwin-Felts detectives, as well as those who joined simply because they were itching for a fight. Maybe they wanted to experience the thrill of battle one more time. Maybe they knew this conflict would be some heavy stuff. All in all, Don Chafin assembled a formidable army, though much smaller than the unionized miners marching from the North. Regardless of the size of either army, Don Chafin was privileged to control superior fire power, the high ground of Blair Mountain, and a pretty full sack of combat experienced fighters. Over the three days of battle, it's estimated over three million rounds of ammunition were fired. That's a million rounds per day. And this took place on American soil, between American citizens. To me, it was as serious as any Civil War battle. It just didn't get the press it deserved.

Whether or not the average marching miner was aware, (most were), the whole affair was triggered by the murder of Sid Hatfield in Welch about 30 days earlier. They all had enough of the brutal tactics of Baldwin-Felts detective agency, Don Chafin and the do-nothing representatives in Charleston. By September 1921, the brutality of the mining companies had been ongoing for over 30 years. The Battle of Blair Mountain was the culmination of years of oppression and domination. To assemble over 6,000 men in a narrow valley in Kanawha County, and march them 60+ miles over incredibly difficult terrain could only happen once in a lifetime. Why would you grab your rifle and join a force that was destined to lose? You wouldn't. Did you know you would march for a week to assault a mountain with machine guns on the top? Were you duped by your leaders, or were you so desperate that it no longer mattered? I believe the never-ending injustice and the total disregard of human decency prompted these men to say, more or less, "The hell with it. What have I got to lose? If they can commit murder and get away with it, then what chance do I have? To Mingo!"

This pic is approximately one mile upstream on Lens Creek near Hernshaw, WV. Imagine 6,000 + miners marching up this narrow valley. They must have been stretched out for over a mile, probably more. Maybe a lot more. The road was neither paved, nor this wide at this time. It would have been best suited for a horse and rider in 1921.

The Shooting Begins

Early in the morning of September 1st, 1921, an advance force of miners moved into the Trace Creek area, east of Sharples, West Virginia, on what is now St. Rte. 17. This road is now historically named Blair Mountain Hwy. It is just north of the battle site. During this movement, there was a skirmish with a small outpost of Chafin's army, mostly mine guards, but several state troopers as well. The trooper's presence was enough to make it recognized by the government. The miners killed three sheriff's deputies and took several prisoners. One miner was killed. This shootout made it deadly serious. Over the next two days, most of the action was positioning, provision placement, and constant sniper fire. The miners lacked any pretense of high ground. Every flank was guarded, and every high position was armed. The miners were facing an uphill battle. To make it worse, Don Chafin hired several commercial airplane pilots to drop bombs on the approaching miners. A bi-wing WW1 fighter plane managed to drop live mortars on the front lines of the miners. Their efforts were ineffective, but this marked a significant event in American history. This was the first time Americans intentionally tried to bomb other Americans from an airplane, on American soil. It has not happened since, as far as I can find.

On September 3rd, an onslaught of 3,000 miners began the general advance up the slopes of Blair Mountain. Their old machine gun rattled off rounds from the base of the mountain. It is seldom a good deployment to be aiming uphill. The pop, pop, pop of rifle rounds was as intense as any battle in any war. This engagement continued for about three hours. By noon, the miners retreated, having gained zero ground. Soon after, fresher troops were mustered to the front, and the fighting resumed. This push was initiated along the entire front of the defense--at least five miles. Again, the miners could not reach the top of the mountain and were forced to retreat. A doctor for Chafin's army, Dr. Miliken, who had fought in the Spanish-American war, said he heard about as much gunfire as he heard in Manila. (H.B. Lee) So, these were real battles. Real men died on both sides, though

Built in 1901, the George Thornburg House is part of the US National Register of Historic Places--1991. It is located at the corner of Main St. and Central Ave. in Barboursville, WV. After Mr. Thornburg's death in 1927, the building was converted into dormitory rooms for students attending Morris Harvey College, located directly across Central Ave. General Bandholtz, with his 2000 regulars, would have passed by this home in August of 1921. What a sight that must have been.

Main St. Barboursville, WV. Part of the old James River Turnpike. General Bandholtz marched his 2,000 regulars down this street in the late Summer of 1921. The grassy area was once the campus of Morris Harvey College.

the true number of casualties will probably never be known. After the second retreat, the tide of the battle was about to turn against the miners. General Bandholtz was about to make his return appearance to Southern West Virginia. I doubt he was happy about that.

Barboursville, West Virginia sits on the confluence of the Mud and Guyandotte rivers. (I fished there many times in my youth.) Unknown to the miners, Bandholtz was commanding 2,000 federal troops. They were U.S Army Reserves—real soldiers. He mustered his troops in the small town of Barboursville and promptly divided his forces. Half of the regulars followed Major Smart up the Coal River, to the southeast. The destination was to form in the rear of the advancing miners. The other half, which Bandholtz led, marched up the Guyandotte River. This route was mostly south. This positioning would place both battalions in the rear of the miners' advance. They arrived just after the second retreat by the miners in late afternoon, September 3rd, 1921. I wouldn't want to be the messenger who had to report this news to Bill Blizzard. That would have been hard to do. Knowing the terrain, this had to be a very fast march to cover this much distance in such a short time.

Don Chafin had approximately 3,000 men defending the top of Blair Mountain. Bill Blizzard had somewhere between 6,000 and 7,000 miners at the base of the mountain. Add the federal troops, and you had between 9,000 - 10,000 men, all with guns, crammed into a few square miles of rugged Logan County. It is nothing short of a miracle that the number of casualties didn't run into the hundreds, if not the thousands. My best guess is somewhere around 100 men died, from both sides. History will never reveal the true number of casualties from this battle.

Because of the absolute hatred of the mine guards, Baldwin-Felts in particular, I believe the miners would have eventually breached the top of Blair Mountain and awful hand-to-hand combat would have happened. Whether or not they could have invaded Logan is in doubt. Even though the miners were outgunned, they out-numbered Chafin's men at least two to one. They were clearly prepared to die for their cause. Were it not for the arrival of federal troops, I think the potential outcome of this real battle could have been very different. The miners were prepared to die for their cause. Short of assured annihilation, they probably would have pushed on until the last man was standing.

General Bandholtz had trapped the miners with no possible escape route. He demanded they disarm, and they had no other choice. Most of their weapons were confiscated, but many miners hid their arms in the nooks and crannies of the slopes of Blair Mountain. They would return sometime later to retrieve them. The miners were repelled twice on September 3rd, but in each advance, they moved closer and closer to the front lines on the crest of this well defended mountain. Though they were very close to seeing Don Chafin's army eye to eye, they could not have known about the arrival of the General from Manilla. Bill Blizzard's army would fall to defeat. The atonement for Sid's murder would have to wait awhile.

Alas, Don Chafin would go on to reign supreme in Logan County for another three long years. Blair Mountain was the miners' Gettysburg, or better yet, Stones River. The tide had turned for the worse, but the war was nowhere close to done. Neither side was willing to capitulate. As the smoke from the battle of Blair Mountain dissipated into the clouds, life for the miners returned to its dismal same. The era of investigation soon took root. The state of West Virginia needed a fall guy to try and convict for the loss and expense of the battle. They should have looked no further than sheriff Don Chafin. But he was way too powerful, and he had too many allies to pursue. Thus, the weaker candidates could only be found within the union movement. And that's exactly what happened. And, of course, the black money to fund these investigations would come from the coal companies. (I can't prove that.) But there's no doubt, collectively, they had much deeper pockets than the UMWA. They only needed the right lawyers. They already owned the right judges. Just like the set-up of Sid's murder in Welch, the machine of the mining companies and the corrupt politicians persuaded two union supporters to become union antagonizers. To me, that's a hard gut-check. But I guess it was the money. It's always the money.

The Lawyers

C. W. Osenton and A. M. Belcher, two well paid attorneys from Huntington, WV, had been supporters of the miners' movement for many years. They were commonly referred to as the "Coal Dust Twins." (H.B. Lee) These lawyers represented the miners after the Paint Creek disaster in 1913, and well beyond that. They must have been effective because the mining companies offered them more money than the UMWA could muster. They were tasked with proving that the leaders committed treason by directing the miners to march to Blair Mountain. And, because men died in this conflict, the charge of murder would be applied, as well. Treason and murder . . . WOW! The common miner could not have envisioned these charges when he met up at Marmet.

Can you imagine what Bill Blizzard, Frank Keeney, Fred Mooney, and Bill Petrey thought of these turncoats? They were deliberately stabbed in the back. Even if they were guilty of these crimes, how could an eternal ally so blatantly switch sides for a bigger bag of cash? But, they did. After a Grand Jury was convened in Logan County, they indicted the UMWA leadership, and 525 marchers, for treason and murder. (H.B. Lee) The treason charge was for waging war against the state of West Virginia. A month later, 210 more miners were indicted by a grand jury from the same jurisdiction. Altogether, 735 miners were charged with treason and murder. The majority of these poor miners marched up Lens Creek and beyond with no concept they would be charged with such a serious crime. If you truly believe you're doing the right thing, and then you are charged with treason, how must that have felt?

These miners were poor and poorly educated. They were the hardworking salt of the Earth. However, they were anything but dumb. There's no way they could have known they would be charged with treason during the onset of the march. Though they were incited by the union leadership, they had been pushed to the limit by the clearly unconstitutional tactics of the Baldwin-Felts agency, the WV State Government and, in particular, Logan County Sheriff Don Chafin. Their justified hatred of these entities needed only a casual push to make international history by 1921. The idea of treason could not have entered their minds. They were intent on justice, even if their tactics lacked due process. I'm not saying I agree with this, but it was deadly serious by this time. The oversight of jurisprudence should make clear that reasonable men can be coerced to do unreasonable things given a sustained lack of humanity. The real criminals would not be charged. But, some of the real patriots would be.

The charges against Bill Blizzard (the general), Frank Keeney, Fred Mooney, and Bill Petrey were lodged in Logan County--Don Chafin's jurisdiction. In addition, Keeney and Mooney were indicted in Mingo County. The charge was accessory to murder. These four men were the real target of the mine operators, the WV State government and Don Chafin. The remainder of the 735 miners were of much lower value.

The UMWA hired a lawyer named Tom Townsend, who was a very capable man from the capitol of Charleston. His aid was Harold Houston. Together, they initiated what was basically a "go-fund-me" account to help defend their clients. They quickly raised over $50,000 for their defense. Adjusting for inflation, this amount would be the equivalent of more than $600,000 in today's dollars. They were able to have the prisoners transferred to Kanawha County by convening another grand jury in that county. Effectively, these snap lawyers precipitated the indictments of the UMWA leaders in a county where Don Chafin had no jurisdiction. They moved quickly. The prisoners were transferred to the Kanawha County jail, far away from the grasp of Don Chafin.

Frank and Fred were removed from the Logan jail. They were transferred to Kanawha County, which bypassed Don Chafin altogether. The same was true for Bill Blizzard and Bill Petrey. However, in a remarkable circumstance, these UMWA leaders realized they had played the system for their own sake. They understood the other miners held captive (in Logan County) did not have the same privileges as they did. They decided that their credibility as leaders was contingent upon the support of the masses. They made contact with Don Chafin and offered their surrender if he assured their personal protection. The UMWA leaders and Don Chafin agreed to meet in Huntington. The UMWA heavyweights agreed to be transported back to the Logan County jail. Agree or disagree with the circumstances, that took guts. They had to know they were likely to be murdered. And yet, they made this call.

For the next 59 days, these four men were held on the top floor of the Logan jail. They expected to be killed at any moment. But, on day 60, for reasons unknown, Don Chafin agreed to send the miners' trial to a different jurisdiction. Their chances of living went up 500 percent. The new trial would take place in Charles Town, WV. This is the county seat of Jefferson County. It's also the town where John Brown was tried, convicted and hanged in 1859. Altogether, 1,000 defendants would descend on this hamlet for final judgement of the Blair Mountain catastrophe. Every B&B, hotel, and public accommodation was filled. The town was standing room only.

John Marshall Woods was the presiding judge in this historic case. The "Coal Dust Twins" (Osenton and Belcher) were the prosecuting attorneys for the state. Townsend was the defending attorney for the miners. During the opening proceedings, attorney Owenston was loud and boisterous. Soon after the trial began, the judge informed counsel that no one present had trouble hearing, and to keep his arguments to a decibel common for all. This admonishment took much of Osenton's vigor away. His style was stymied, and this removed much of his wind. This was very good fortune for Mr. Blizzard.

At some early time in the trial, the defense demanded separate trials for the 1,000 defendants. The state argued this change in venue would take 50 years to complete, but the request was quite constitutional. One of the defendants, a lowly miner who fired his rifle uphill with the rest of the soldiers, asked the judge for a word. Judge Woods granted his request to speak to the court. "Your honor, I'm one of the defendants. We agree it will take 50 years to try all these cases. If it's all the same to you, Sir, I'd like my case tried last." (H.B. Lee)

As the trial fiasco proceeded, Bill Blizzard was accused of being the "general" in command. The prosecution charged he had his boots on the ground at Blair Mountain and was in total control of the troop's movements. These charges were supported by many miners who were present at the battle. I speculate these prosecution witnesses were anticipating leniency regarding their sentencing if convicted. However, Blizzard's co-defendants testified he was never on the battlefield, but rather in the UMWA Headquarters in Charleston during the struggle.

Matewan Jail and city hall, 1908. Of all the towns I visited to write this book, this is the only original jail I could find from the era. I'm sure there are others. Many have all been replaced some years ago. This jail is restored to its original condition. This is super cool history. I'm not sure how you could put more than three or four detainees into this jail. It's really small. The town of Matewan did a great job restoring this building to its original condition.

I believe he was in Charleston. Regardless, Bill Blizzard was acquitted, but I believe he would have made a more historic mark had he been found guilty. I believe he really tried to do the right thing given the circumstances. But, yes, legally, he did facilitate treason. And yes, he was responsible for the coordination of thousands of armed rebels. They marched against a duly elected government. These were serious charges.

Upon acquittal, a wild celebration broke out, and Bill Blizzard was carried out of the courthouse on the shoulders of the miners. They initiated a parade through Charles Town. Blizzard, much the same as Sid Hatfield, had courage and stood up to the powers that persecuted the common miner. Many citizens respected his bravery, and many despised him and considered him a criminal. The state was as polarized as our nation is today. Because of all this unrest, the mine owners and operators were more than alarmed. Collectively, they eliminated Sid Hatfield and Ed Chambers. They repelled an invasion and won a significant battle. They funded the prosecution of the UMWA leadership, but then fell completely flat. They spent a fortune. Frank Keeney had his venue moved to yet another county, but the momentum was so in favor of the union leadership that the charges were dropped, and no trial took place. It all fizzled. Hundreds of people died but, ultimately, the coal operators were right back to where they started—nowhere. These moguls remained faceless and unknown. They did, however, create a couple legends. Namely, Sid Hatfield and Bill Blizzard.

The Saber is in the Scabbard

The UMWA was very different in 1921. There was an essence of virtue then. The goal was about basic human rights as well as basic working rights. Bill Blizzard did this deed without expectation of fame or money. So did Sid. He enjoyed the support of like-minded followers much the same as we do today. He had skin in the game. I would hope the current Union leadership will resume that spirit that they had in the 1920's. Unfortunately, I think they are simply consumed with power, just like everyone else today. Power in the 1920's, in Mingo and Logan Counties was consolidated by the entity that had the most money. In that time, the entity was the coal and railroad companies. The forces from that era have since been replaced. Those forces that the miners hated in 1920 are gone forever. Those puppeteers have long since disappeared, but the game is eternally similar. The only thing that remains the same is the human spirit to help your neighbor and your community. God help us if we lose that spirit.

By the end of 1923, the trials from Blair Mountain were all but over. The new president of the UMWA, John L. Lewis, banished all the former leadership in District 17. He was very upset that Blizzard, Keeney, Mooney, and Petrey did not confer with him prior to their incitement. He appointed Percy Tetlow as district president. Yet, the union in Mingo and Logan counties was all but dead due to the proliferation of the hated "yellow dog" contracts. Not only were the mine operators back to square one, so was the union. All the while, the Baldwin-Felts detectives were wreaking havoc just as they had before. All that for nothing. Hence, it was an era I call the bittersweet years.

The sheriff of Logan County, Don Chafin, was nearing the end of his reign. In 1924, he was arrested for moonshining. He was tried and convicted by his peers. After his appeal was denied in 1925, he spent two years in prison near Atlanta, GA. After release, he maintained his connections to the Democratic Party of WV and also became a lobbyist for the coal companies. Though he was officially a felon, he was considered a hero in the eyes of the mine operators. He spent much time in the capitol of Charleston as his influence in Logan County had evaporated to his political opponents. In 1936, he formally moved to Huntington. Not long after, he purchased the entire Pritchard building for $400,000. He was worth millions. I don't know how a county sheriff can become a millionaire from public service, especially after two years in federal prison. But he was rich beyond imagination for the time. He renovated the top floor of the building and lived large. He died from a series of heart attacks on August 9th, 1954. He was 67 years old.

PART 3: THE BITTERSWEET YEARS

ꙮ Last Gasps of a Dynasty ꙮ

Between 1925 and 1927, America was governed by President Calvin Coolidge and the 69th Congress. Republicans, in the house held a solid majority with 247 members. The roaring 20's was in full swing. So too was the Baldwin-Felts detective agency. Life for the average miner in Southern West Virginia was little changed from the recently concluded mine war. There was sparse federal oversight resulting from these battles and skirmishes. The miners were still completely controlled by the mining companies, Thomas Felts and William Baldwin had won all the battles to date. About the only difference was the demise of Don Chafin in Logan County, but that didn't help anybody in Mingo County.

There were still long tons and short tons. There was still payment in company script. There were still "company" stores that only accepted script for payment. There was still abject poverty and repression by the mining companies and their proxies. I imagine this time frame as being the most depressing ever for the miners. After "all that," there was still nothing significant that changed for the lives of the miners. Sid was dead and Blair Mountain was a bust. William Baldwin and Thomas Felts must have been quite content by now. But the wheels of justice were beginning to get some unexpected grease.

In 1926, Congress passed the Railway Labor Act. This act found its origins in 1877 after the Great Railroad Strike that started in Martinsburg, West Virginia and bled over to several other states. Basically, it created a Board of Mediation (later a National Board of Mediation) that attempted to avoid strikes through arbitration and mediation. A predecessor of this law was the Erdman Act of 1898. This law prohibited discrimination against employees who were involved in union activities.

It also, more significantly, prohibited a railroad company from using "yellow dog" contracts as a condition of employment. While these laws did nothing for the immediate future of the coal miners, at least they set the precedent for future laws that would help them.

The Erdman Act remained intact until 1906. However, a labor incident involving a master mechanic with the Louisville and Nashville Railroad would soon change this act forever. William Adair fired an employee he supervised for his activities in a labor union known as the Order of Locomotive Firemen. The man he fired was O. B. Coppage. This firing was in direct violation of the Erdman Act. Adair was indicted by the Eastern Kentucky District Court and fined $100. Adair eventually appealed to the Supreme Court. In a 6-2 decision, the Supreme Court held that the Erdman Act was unconstitutional. The court found the "due process" clause of the 5th Amendment to the Constitution prohibits an invasion of personal liberty, as well as the right of property. They concluded that the company had a right to make a contract for the purchase of labor, and also, the worker had the same right to sell his labor. The government, state or Federal, could not infringe on the private contract between the employee and the employer. This era of labor and the unionization movement in America became known as the Lochner Era.

As part of the Erdman Act decision, Justice John Harlan cited the landmark Lochner v. New York labor decision of 1905. In this decision, 5-4, the court held that a company could require their employees to work 10 hours a day, or up to 60 hours per week. They cited the 14th Amendment's "due process" clause. (First the 5th Amendment, and also the 14th Amendment). They provided it allowed a company to enjoy a "freedom of contract" with their workers. In other words, the employee agreed to the terms of employment prior to accepting the job. This was a horrible decision that lasted (in essence) until 1937. Justice Oliver Wendell Holmes wrote a three-paragraph dissent decrying the use of the "due process" clause. He called it "judicial activism." These decisions created a powerful condition in 1920 Matewan. Sid Hatfield would cross the Tug River without any knowledge of these events. But, he would surely have to deal with them.

Completed in 1925, the Pritchard Building in Huntington, WV stands at 13 floors. Don Chafin lived on the top floor. He created the first "penthouse" in Huntington. He purchased this magnificent architecture for $400,000 in 1938. He paid cash. He was well liked in Huntington because he tipped very nicely. These were the heydays in the City of Huntington, WV. Don lived well.

Script money from the New River Smokeless Coal Co. This photo is a complement of the Matewan Visitor's Center. You can view a wide array of "script" coins there.

Thacker Coal Co. script. One of many examples you can view at the Visitor's Center in Matewan, WV.

Patience, Dear Miner

Between 1926 and 1932, there were no significant labor laws passed by Congress. It was the Roaring 20's and America had no time to tap the breaks on production. The Baldwin-Felts detective agency was free to operate within the existing laws of the era. This time was soon to end and the Great Depression was about to begin. Unfortunately, most of these landmark decisions were passed without benefiting the coal miners in Southern West Virginia. As the coal continually flowed out of the mountains, the furnaces and boilers of America's industrial might demanded ever more black rock. Many new innovations were rapidly introduced by the inventors and creators of America, and beyond. Most of which were dependent on the never-ending supply of coal. This coal produced the stuff we take for granted every day. It still does, but to a lesser degree than even a few years ago.

During the Roaring 20's, much of America was acquainting itself with new marvels that enhanced our lives. In 1923, the first instant camera was developed. Also that year, the first bulldozer was introduced to the world. In 1924, the radio altimeter was invented, allowing an aircraft to judge its altitude. 1926 saw the first electric garage door opener. (The people of Matewan would have little use for this invention.) In 1927, the bread slicer, the jukebox, and the pressure washer came to be. The electric razor emerged in 1928, as did penicillin. Sunglasses first hit the beach in 1929. Also that year, frozen food was invented by Clarence Birdseye. All these inventions, and many more, emerged while the average coal miner worked countless hours in a black hole somewhere in Appalachia. Like the long shadows of late September, the joy and excitement of the American experience could not penetrate the valleys of Mingo. It seemed that tomorrow would always be like yesterday. As I often say, it's the same as it was tomorrow.

On October 24th, 1929, a Thursday, the roaring 20's came to an abrupt end. In a four day stretch, starting with Black Thursday, the Dow Jones Industrial Average lost $30 billion in value. This was 25% of the market's total value. If inflation remained the same, that value today would be $441 billion. The demand for coal, sunglasses, bulldozers and altimeters would tank, and fast. Beginning in 1922, the NYSE gained an average of 20% per year. Many investors were buying "on margin." They did this for almost a decade. This is no different than the average citizen buying stuff they can't afford with a credit card today. But in 1929, there were no Federal safeguards to protect the avid investor from financial ruin. More than a few investors jumped to their death from tall buildings in 1930. The average miner in Mingo County, WV showed up for work as usual. Most had no idea what these events meant to their future. Most did not have the time to care. They just kept digging coal, like they always had. Baldwin-Felts detectives were still ensuring these miners remained non-union. Much of America had changed almost overnight. But for the average miner in Matewan, nothing had noticeably changed. And so it was. But, in 1932, eleven long years after Sid was murdered, and three years after the stock market crash, Congress began enacting a series of labor legislation that Sid could have only dreamed about. The pendulum was beginning to swing the other way for organized labor.

In the twilight months of President Herbert Hoover's administration, he signed the Norris-Laguardia Act on March 23rd, 1932. The vote tally was incredibly one-sided when compared to a controversial bill today; 75-5 in the Senate and 363-13 in the House. First proposed in 1928, this act would provide relief to the labor unions and the union members against the unfair practices of many corporations. First, it basically outlawed the hated "yellow-dog" contracts. Second, it stripped the federal courts from issuing an injunction against striking workers if their actions were peaceful. This is significant because big business frequently used this tactic to cripple the labor union, at the onset of a dispute, before it could gain any momentum. The mining company (or any industrial giant) would find a friendly court to rule against the union when a labor dispute was in its earliest stage. This would be similar to preventing the instant replay rule in football. Imagine the coach disputes a referee's call and asks for a review. As soon as the process gets started, the owners, with much deeper pockets, demand the play stands as called, if it benefits them. The replay process is stopped (basically an injunction) and the game goes on. Both Republicans and Democrats agreed this was completely unfair. But it only happened because of a shifting public sentiment that forced both sides to meet and agree to do something. This sentiment developed over a very long period of time. The injustice of Sid's era was only a part of this act. Many other workers, in many other industries, faced similar circumstances. For the record, Herbert Hoover was a Republican.

The Norris-Laguardia act was quite libertarian, in my opinion. It more or less removed the federal courts from the labor dispute process, thereby allowing the free market to decide the outcome. It was a short-sighted bandaid for a severe laceration. I look at it as the final breath of the Lochner era. The "hands-off" approach by the federal government forced it to rethink its labor philosophy. Manufacturing and mining were still growing in spite of the Great Depression, at least through early 1933. Strikes were all too common and virtually no one emerged a winner. Washington needed something more, something with teeth. It needed something that neither side would embrace fully, but both sides could tolerate. Sid would have been encouraged by the effort, but Laguardia was flawed legislation. Even so, it is still a valid law in America and was used as recently as 1982.

Between mid-1932 and 1935, the unions and the corporations were allowed to "slug it out." On March 4th, 1933, Franklin D. Roosevelt, became the 32nd president of the United States. This year would see a significant uptick in union organizing, strikes and strike breaking by corporations. In the first year of the FDR administration, the Great Depression was in full swing. The FDR administration was far more sympathetic to the union effort, but it was torn by the potential effects of destabilizing an already fragile economy by endorsing labor policies that were heretofore unpracticed, by and large. It was a delicate balance to both rev the economy and assuage the populace that elected him. A different approach was needed. Laguardia was the law of the land, but FDR needed something to bridge the gap between the free market and federal oversight. He was forced into supporting legislation that was far more capitalistic than his instincts would normally bear—in my opinion. I believe he was desperate for middle ground, and he took bad advice from his advisors. As the strikes and labor disputes continued, he pressed his advisors to supply new ideas for new legislation. He was in a hurry. That's when you make mistakes. He didn't make the same mistake twice throughout his administrations.

The Final Stretch to Overtime

The Norris-Laguardia Act survived judicial scrutiny, but after three short years it was usurped by the National Recovery Act of 1935. But before that, in June 1933, FDR signed the National Industrial Recovery Act (NIRA), which would soon be found unconstitutional by the Supreme Court. This act was a major swing to the federal government's side. It tried to regulate wages and prices, but instead, it was costing FDR a significant amount of support. The act even backdoored the formation of certain monopolies. This legislation was a swing too far the other way. Rather than stimulate the economy, it had the opposite effect. On May 27th, 1935, in Schechter Poultry Corp. vs. United States, the Supreme Court handed FDR a major defeat. The NIRA was no more. No matter, it was now full steam ahead to the New Deal.

On July 6th, 1935, FDR and the 74th Congress finally got a base hit for organized labor. Also known as the Wagnor Act, this legislation finally guaranteed a private union the right to organize and collectively bargain. This law established the National Labor Relations Board, or the NLRB. This board is still quite active in America today. It's one of FDR's many legacies. It promotes freedom of association among the employees, freedom to choose their representatives, and the labor disputes that reach this board are decided in binding arbitration. It's rather like the Supreme Court of labor. Originally staffed by three members, chosen by the POTUS, the board was expanded to five members in 1947 and remains that way today. Excluding alternative members selected to fill unexpected voids, the members are appointed to five-year terms. The political persuasion of the members tends to follow the party of the president in power. Sid Hatfield may not have imagined an entity so favorable to his cause in 1921. Even so, it was not the end of the conflict. There were still many problems between the corporations and the workers. And, at the time of enactment, the private trade unions still had their share of problems. There was much more yet to come.

In 1935, the unemployment rate in America was 20.1%. (The Balance.com) In 1933, the rate was 24.9%. The economy was still in a depression. Put another way, there were 11.3 million people unemployed. Having a union was all fine and well, but if there are no jobs, what does it matter? Compare that to January 2020, when there were only 5.9 million Americans unemployed. The US population between then and now is two to three-fold. So, if the Census Bureau claims we have ~327,000,000 citizens today (likely more), consider we had ~127,000,000 citizens in 1935, which is still twice the population of Great Britain today. Yet, in 1935, America had over five million more workers unemployed than today (pre-Covid 19). And, we've added over 100% more citizens to our country since then. Can you imagine what 20 to 25% unemployment would look like today? With our current national debt of over $27 trillion, it could easily collapse our nation. Just like the Roaring 20's, our government is "buying on margin" and spending with reckless abandon. A market correction today has more than twice the potential devastation than in 1929, even with the FDIC, SIPC and all the other insurance acts or agencies of today. But, that's a completely different story.

1935 was the last year the Baldwin-Felts detective agency would remain intact. Their whole mission of preventing unionization was now prohibited by federal law. William Gibboney Baldwin would die a year later, and Thomas Felts would follow the next year, in 1937 (Lon Savage, E-WV). Their company, or anything like it, will forever remain in the dustbin of regrettable American history. Like slavery, Jim Crow, women's suffrage, or even Korematsu vs. US, our nation has had its share of challenges to the Bill of Rights. Baldwin-Felts was the result of a natural progression in the business cycle of the time. There was an unfulfilled business need that Baldwin exploited. He wasn't breaking any federal laws, and that's the problem. This case demonstrates that America is ever evolving. It took over 40 years for Congress to recognize the right of the worker to legally organize. Actually, it could be argued that it was much longer than that. Sid Hatfield would have been glorified had he remained alive in 1935. He would have been in his mid-40's. Unfortunately, he was somewhat forgotten by this time. But congress wasn't done. What came next would have been unthinkable to Sid.

Finally, Overtime

On June 14th, 1938, FDR signed the Fair Labor Standards Act. I will refer to this law as FLSA henceforth. For the first time in American history, federal law established a 40-hour work week. Any hours worked over that threshold would be paid at 1 ½ times the regular rate of pay. FLSA also mandates a minimum wage. In 1938, that rate was .25 cents per hour. (That is about $4.55 today if adjusted for inflation.) As of today, the minimum wage rate is $7.50 per hour. Good luck trying to hire someone at that rate. FLSA continued with strict regulation of workers under the age of 16. Hence, child labor laws were enacted for the first time ever. The last significant component required the business to maintain record keeping, such as time cards. This would prevent the employer from cheating the worker by claiming he or she worked less than claimed. None of these conditions were common in Sid's day, in Mingo and anywhere else in southern West Virginia. I can only imagine how excited he would have been to enjoy this law and the Wagnor Act, as well. But then, had these laws been created when Sid crossed the Tug, there would not have existed the Baldwin-Felts detective agency. Neither would there have been a Sid Hatfield. He would have been just another small-town chief of police, or maybe just a blacksmith. If so, he may have been able to die of old age, like Charles E. Lively did.

So clearly, Sid's role in these laws is not because of him alone. He was just a significant footnote in the great labor dispute. Though his legacy was profound, there were many others like him in the labor movement. From the inception of the AFL in December 1886, and up to 1938, the labor movement in America caused the deaths of hundreds of workers. Even Senator Robert F. Wagnor, sponsor of the Wagnor Act, was fired upon in Portland, Oregon in 1935. In this altercation with striking longshoremen, a young college student,

James Conner, was shot and killed. He had just married and was working as a strikebreaker to earn extra money while on vacation. Between 1871 and 1938, including railroads, mines, textile workers, longshoremen, meat packers, agricultural workers, streetcar workers, auto workers, and ever cigar makers, approximately 836 workers were killed in labor disputes. This number is probably on the low end. In most cases, the strikers' union was not recognized by the federal government. Sid Hatfield and Ed Chambers, as well as Cabell Testerman, are included in this number.

Some of the other names included in these confrontations are Luka Vahernik and Louis Tikas. Luka was shot in the head in the Ludlow, Colorado strike in April 1914. 177 heavily armed mine guards fired a machine gun into the miners' tent camp. Afterwards, they set the camp on fire. When the shooting was done, five miners, two women, and 12 children lay dead. The machine gun was courtesy of Baldwin-Felts, specifically, Albert and Lee Felts. The train car was none other than the Death Special. The mine was owned by John D. Rockefeller, Jr. It was just another bloody mess where no one was held accountable. That stuff could never happen today. At least, I hope not.

Coal miner Cesco Estep was killed in the Paint Creek, Cabin Creek disaster near Charleston, WV in 1913. Again, the Death Special fired directly into a picket line. Cesco was the only casualty. After the dispute ended, many workers perished, including women and children, from starvation and exposure. Combined with Blair Mountain, these three incidents produced the second greatest number of fatalities in this era. However, the worst example was the Great Railroad Strike of 1877. In this multi-state strike that began in Martinsville, WV on July 14th, at least 112 strikers were killed. It was the first national strike in American history. The battles occurred in West Virginia, Pennsylvania, New York, Illinois, and Maryland. Baldwin-Felts was not a part of this strike. William G. Baldwin was only 17 years old when these events happened. Still, I'm fairly sure they had a considerable influence on his young life. George Armstrong Custer died at Little

BigHorn about one year earlier. It was a violent time in our American experience, and I believe William Baldwin was well accustomed to violence by the time he formed his company.

The last example comes from Thibodaux, Louisannia. Between November 5th and November 23rd, 1887, sugar cane workers (90% African American) were systematically murdered by the Louisiana State Militia. Most members of the militia were active National Guardsmen, but a good number were nothing more than prominent citizens. The workers were trying to join a union called the Knights of Labor. Their demand was simply one more dollar per day in pay. Altogether, 10,000 laborers formed the general strike. At least 57 workers were killed during this dispute. That number is probably on the low side as well. Shallow graves were discovered on the outskirts of town for many weeks to follow. The difference in this incident was that it was racially connected. A labor dispute is one thing, but in the Jim Crow era of Louisannia, race was a considerable factor as well. Either way, there was no justification for killing this many people. As usual, no member of the militia was arrested, tried or convicted, just like Mingo. After the unrest, things just went on as before, minus 57 more citizens. This incident probably stifled the African American communities' attempt at unionization. By 1903, African American membership in unions was less than 3% of total membership. (History.com)

⤶ Harry's Veto Overturned ⤷

In 1939, two of the greatest movies ever produced hit the big screens of America. Gone with the Wind and the Wizard of Oz set records that are still unmatched in movie history. Gone with the Wind received 10 Academy Awards and Wizard of OZ received six. The Great Depression was still on-going, but the wild success of these movies symbolized the mood of many Americans. It's as though the masses sensed the beginning of the end of this dark period. And so, it was a chance to switch off their worries and concerns for at least a few hours. The budgets for these two movies were bold. Over $3 million for Wizard of Oz. It was more for Gone with the Wind.

The advertising budgets that followed were prescient. These two films brought the movie industry out of the depression sooner than most other industries. The gross receipts eclipsed anything Hollywood had ever seen. It also enhanced their ability to influence the entire nation like never before. The vast amount of money spent to produce these films was ambitious. The payoff was magnificent. Though neither was the first color movie, they were the first color films seen by millions of people, worldwide. The change of a movie from black and white to color is quite symbolic, especially in this tumultuous era. To me, it's symbolic of the changing dynamic of life for the average American. I can only imagine the spirit of the audience leaving the theater after watching either of these two, epic movies. I think of it as the sun coming out after 40 days of rain.

And with the labor unions, there was a sense of hope in the air that they would be fully recognized by our American government, and the American citizens as well. But, alas, hope can be a dangerous expectation. 1939 was a short year after the Fair Labor Standards Act changed everything for the unions. It was also the year Adolph Hitler swept through Poland. The sun was finally out, but dark clouds were swelling just beyond the horizon.

Gone were Baldwin-Felts and their henchmen. Gone was the Death Special. Gone was the short ton vs. the long ton. However, what lay ahead was yet more strife and struggle for the unions. The onset of WWII effectively ended the Great Depression in late 1941. American manufacturing was at its zenith during the war and for many years to come. The US automobile companies were growing leaps and bounds both during the war and after. The steel industry was booming. The highest density of union membership, a percent of the labor force, was in 1954. (Bureau of Labor Statistics) This year, 35% of the private sector working force was represented by a union. Coal mining in WV was not yet fully automated and the global demand was still very high. Hence, they still needed a lot of laborers. This was the golden age of mining in WV, as far as production and employment was concerned.

It was also a time of environmental devastation to the mountain tops, the rivers and streams of the state, but that's also another story. Never again would a gang of brown shirts invade a town and threaten the common folk with violence. Those days were gone with the wind. However, new threats would replace the omnipresence of William Baldwin and Thomas Felts in Mingo County. And, they would come from the very people who were once helpful.

In 1947, if Sid Hatfield were still alive, I believe he would have been an icon to the labor movement. He might have been more famous than John L Lewis had he remained alive. Remember, he killed Albert Felts. He would have been about 54 years old by this time. His capacity and role would be totally different, but he would still have a pistol tucked in his pants, or vest, or around his ankle. He would have been riding high with the passage of the Fair Labor Standards Act. Conditions had been favorable for the unions for over a decade, but equilibrium is a powerful force. The will of the majority in America will always prevail so long as we remain a representative republic government. So, something was about to go terribly wrong for the growth of the unions in 1947.

After the death of FDR, victory in Europe, the nuclear bombing of Japan, and the end of WWII, America was governed by the man that said, "The buck stops here." We were suddenly in the ether land between Constitutional rule and a purer form of democracy. He would have continued the style of governing of FDR, and why not? It could have gone either way. I'm not saying a former President was against the Constitution. This event was just a natural and normal turn to the opposite end of the compass, a normal adjustment, just like we've done for the past 230+ years. That man was Harry S. Truman. He was the president who authorized the nuclear attack on Nagasaki and Hiroshima.

Given the circumstances, I agree with his call. He made that call during an extreme period in our history. Once the war was over, we had to decide what we wanted America to be. 1947 was a fulcrum of our modern government. Congress had been very favorable to the union cause from 1935 until 1947. And then, the Taft-Hartley Act was passed as law. It was a swing back to the will of the majority after 12 years of favorable union legislation, which, I believe, was just and necessary. Again, this was a fast-moving period of American history. We had endured 10+ years of the Great Depression and then four years of horrible warfare, genocide and the rapid rise of communism, Marxism, and fascism throughout the modern world. It was as if the average citizen just stepped off a 15-year political roller coaster ride. First, you catch your breath and then you regain your senses. You say to your fellow riders, "Wow! That was extreme."

Harry S Truman would veto Taft-Hartley. Article 1, Section 7 of the Constitution gives the president this power. But he was overridden by two thirds of both houses of Congress and the law passed on June 23, 1947. The President of the United States hasn't had his veto overridden all that much in our history, but the Framers knew it would happen eventually. The first time was March 3rd, 1845. The president was John Tyler. It was the 28th Congress, (1843-1845), and his veto was to allow appropriations (money) to fund the building of ships for what was basically the early Coast Guard. He had negotiated contracts with private companies to build these ships without consulting Congress. Those funds were not approved by the House of Representatives, so Congress upheld the very same Article and Section of the Constitution (Art 1, Sec 7) that also prohibits the President from spending money that was not initiated by The House. At this particular time in our history, John Tyler was a lame duck president and he wasn't all that popular.

So far, in our American experience, the President has had his veto overridden 111 times. This includes "pocket vetoes," (vetoes that are not addressed by Congress for more than 10 days). Andrew Johnson stands alone with 15 overrides by Congress. (He was also the first impeached President.) Harry S. Truman and Gerald Ford come in second with 12 veto overrides. Franklin D. Roosevelt and Ronald Regan come in third place with nine each. Richard Nixon comes in fourth with seven overrides. Woodrow Wilson was overridden six times and Franklin Pierce and Grover Cleveland were overridden five times. Ulysses S. Grant, Calvin Coolidge and George W. Bush were each overridden four times. For a more modern perspective, Bill Clinton was overridden twice from a total of 36 vetoes. Barack H. Obama issued 12 vetoes, of which none were overridden. Donald J. Trump issued ten vetoes—with no overrides. Of the 2,583 vetoes issued by our presidents since April 30th, 1789, 112 have been overridden by Congress. That's only 4.3%. So, it's a big deal to have a President's veto overturned by Congress. The Founders understood this concept.

The Taft-Hartley Act veto was overridden (and therefore passed) in great part because America was on economic steroids by this time. Also, there were plenty of "blue dog" Democrats in this era who were philosophically pro-growth, regarding our economy. In addition, we had just entered the Cold War with the Soviet Union. The decade of good news for the unions lost its momentum with the passage of this act. After 12 years of pro-union legislation, preceded by about 75 years of anti-union legislation, this act would slam the door on further consolidation of union influence in America, for the most part. Harry

Truman effectively ended the era of one-party rule in America, but not by his choice. He did it through his actions and his decrees. He wasn't wrong in his thinking, he just didn't comprehend the new era that was happening in America, in real time. He was trying to continue a pattern of legislation that worked well during the depression and a great war. But, America was no longer in a depression. We kicked butt in Europe and Asia. We won an awful war and its effects are still significant today. Harry S. Truman never had a chance of reelection. He simply became part of the past. America was "swinging" again. That's the way we like it.

He would be soundly defeated by WWII general Dwight D. Eisenhower (Ike) in late 1952. Harry quietly moved aside, as he should, and the era of "Happy Days" took hold in America. But, Taft-Hartley still rules today, and that's the thing about laws in America. If they are unchanged by Congress, then they are still law--no matter what. That's where we are today and that's how it works in a representative republic government.

Individual states can decide to be an "open shop" or a "closed shop". To me, this is very 10th Amendment stuff, as it should be. I don't believe any entity should be legislatively favored and/or disfavored in America. at any time in our history. I believe we should all rise or fall from the merits of our own deeds, which is a founding priciple of early union efforts. Taft-Hartley ensures this right for the different states. The states are free to decide this issue for themselves. Honestly, I don't know how Sid would have taken this act. I suspect he wouldn't like it much.

What it Means Today

Having worked in retail for most of my life, and much of it in a union shop, I have a unique exposure to the direct effects of the Fair Labor Standards Act. As a manager of many hundreds of people, you have to consider some very basic concepts of coordinated labor, union or otherwise. Each one of your subordinates is a human, and they all have different needs and expectations. The best managers are the ones who follow the company policy, but also empathize with the myriad personalities they direct. Everyone is different, but certain human aspects are common and predictable. You can direct your staff to perform any function imaginable, but you can only be 100% assured your people will faithfully adhere to the two basic functions of employment; they will look at their schedule, and they will check their pay stub. Any other initiative (or directive) you implement is subject to your skills as a manager.

Demanding expectations without understanding the human reaction is a recipe for disaster. People want to be led, but they want their leaders in the same boat they're in. They also function much more efficiently when they understand the "why" behind the direction. I wonder how loose Sid's lips were. Of the many dozens of managers I worked with over the past 30+ years, the ones who spoke the least were the ones that had the least trust among their subordinates. The ones that spoke the most were usually full of crap. In my experience, the ones who remained calm and chose their words carefully, and then spoke freely, were the ones who influenced me the most. Workers want to be led, but they also want to know their leaders' thoughts and opinions, even if they disagree with them. I think Sid did this very well, but I can't prove that. I think he spoke freely, and that worked for the townspeople of

Matewan. But he chose his words carefully. He was one of them. I think that's why so many citizens showed up for his funeral.

The Fair Labor Standards Act, FSLA, established several basic tenets of work in America; a 40-hour work week (hence overtime), a national minimum wage, child labor laws, and time record keeping. One of the most challenging factors in business is writing a schedule that is legal, good for the company, and good for the staff. Even if you only have 10 employees in your company, you have to schedule them within the existing laws and find a way to inspire employee morale as much as possible. (Imagine writing a schedule for 200+ employees.) The rest of this work will review some of my real-life experiences in dealing with this law.

Practical Application

I will begin with the minimum wage element. One of the more fascinating examples of this component is when the federal government raised the minimum wage in 2007 to $5.85 per hour. At that time, I worked for a large grocery chain. Most of my employees were making the previous minimum of $5.15 per hour. They were all union members. So, everyone got a .70 cent raise and everyone was happy. However, all the new hires (after the rate hike) were provided the same, new minimum wage as the existing clerks. Many of these clerks were long term employees. As a result, clerks with experience and seniority suddenly found themselves being paid at the same rate as someone who had no experience and no seniority. This went over like a lead balloon. This was one event that I couldn't explain to my most loyal employees. I wasn't responsible, but I couldn't defer blame. Checkmate. I represented the company.

As a result of this event, I do not believe in a federally mandated minimum wage anymore. I think each state, each county and each city, should be able to set their own minimum wage. I'm OK with a basement. But the roof, and the space in between, should be wholly the decision of local government. Comparable houses in Florida (where I live) cost way more than they do in many states, and way less in others. Should the government mandate a minimum house value regardless of where the house is located? A minimum wage was necessary in Sid's day, and I think it was the right decision for the time. Is that what we still need today?

Next on the list is record keeping. I do not think this portion of FLSA should be changed. However, it's getting very creepy how companies (technology) are performing this function today. Let's start in 1889. That was the year of the first-time clock in America. It was invented and patented by Willard L. Bundy and his brother Harlow. Their company was known as the Bundy Manufacturing Co. This company merged with other companies and eventually became the International Time Recorder Co. The brothers fell distant toward each other, and Harlow created a new Bundy Manufacturing Co. in 1903. In 1907, Willard Bundy passed away and Harlow eventually renamed his company International Business Machines, or IBM in 1924. (Timeco.com)

In the 1980's, I worked as a salesman in the food distribution industry. I serviced both wholesale and retail establishments. One of the tricks of the trade back then was to determine the weekly volume of any given grocery store. The purpose was to make judgements on how best to spend your accrual funds for advertising, promotions and/or new product placement. Those funds were scarce, so you needed a good idea of which account would give the best return on investment. That information was highly guarded and not given to outsiders. So, if you were able to find the time clock, there was usually a timecard holding rack beside (or near) the clock. You would count the number of timecards, discreetly. Later, you would walk the perimeter of the store and determine the total square footage of the sales floor. By dividing the number of timecards into the square footage of the store, you could establish a fairly accurate weekly volume. Even if your number was way off, you could still compare the data among the total of your accounts. Occasionally, you would find a very small store with a higher volume than one with twice (or more) the square footage.

Often the little guy was doing more business than the big guy. This trick is no longer available because everyone has moved to electronic time keeping. Some of them are scary. Sometime in the mid-2000's, the use of the biometric time clock became prevalent. This is the system that verifies your identity through the scanning of your finger. Basically, you are "fingerprinted" by your company. This discouraged any possible mischief from your associates regarding time keeping. Again, this did not go over well initially. I remember training associates with how the system worked. After the time and attendance clerk prepared the associates' data, the associate had to choose one finger to consistently use to clock in or out. Many of them chose their middle finger. I don't disagree with this facet of FLSA. But, with worries about immigration, and for that matter terrorism, I fear what future technology may be introduced. Will they eventually scan our retinas? I hope not.

The third basic tenet of FLSA is child labor laws. Remember in the first decade of the 20th century, Sid Hatfield would have been in his teens. He, like many thousand others, worked six days a week in a coal mine. Many of those days were 10 and even 12 hours long. In 1900, 18% of the American labor force was under the age of 16. (History.com) So, I completely approve of this tenet. Going back to 1912 and 1913, the Paint Creek and Cabin Creek insurrections, the miners made several demands of the mine operators. Those demands included (1) no more blacklisting. (2) miners could join the union. (3) cribbing was to cease. (4) scales were to be installed at every mine to give an accurate account of tonnage mined. (5) compulsory trading at company stores was to cease. (6) docking penalties were to be determined by two checkweighmen. One would be employed by the mining company and the other by the union. All of these demands were rejected, and the ensuing bloodbath went down in history. (King Coal by Stan Cohen)

These were serious and reasonable demands. But I find it curious that child labor reform was not demanded. I can only guess that the practice was so common and widespread, it didn't occur to the miners, and certainly not the mining company. I also believe the miners were so poor and oppressed that they expected the extra income from their children. Many of these kids were paid pennies for a day's work. A common job for a minor was being a "trapper." This job was typically filled by a very young member of the family, and consequently, not the strongest member. Basically, they would sit in total darkness and wait to open wooden doors to allow a coal car to exit the mine. The doors, also known as trap doors, were part of the mine ventilation system. It was common for this shift to last 12 hours.

Other mining jobs were known as the Hurrier and the Thruster. These were very early positions in the mines and their origin comes from Great Britain. In essence, one kid pulled a coal car and the other pushed it. It must have been a horrible and dangerous job. I can only imagine how many years of life were cut short from these poor souls.

Sid Hatfields funeral in Matewan, August 1921. This is an authentic picture. It was provided by a very special person from Matewan. The Nenni Building is on the far right. Look closely and you will see a very long line of people waiting to pay their respects. My guess is this photo was taken from the footbridge over the Tug. There was no floodwall in 1921.

The final tenet of the FLSA is overtime. Any hour worked over 40 in a week will be paid at time and one half. For the average American worker, today is nothing short of a blessing. But for the common miner in 1921, it was a mixed bag of joy. Whereas prior to this new law, a miner could earn more by working longer, even without a minimum wage. The mining companies reacted to the time and a half law by hiring more miners and adding more shifts. Still common today is first shift, swing shift and night shift. All these shifts are eight hours long with a 30-minute lunch break and two 15-minute breaks. Couple that with your newly deducted union dues and a five-day work week, many miners wound up with a smaller paycheck. This is a good example of the "unintended consequences" of finally achieving your ultimate goal. It's not always so simple as your organizers say it is. Still, this law was necessary and benefitted the vast majority of American workers then and certainly today.

It may be a stretch, but I believe the FLSA was directly influenced by the Mine Wars of West Virginia in the early 20th century. There were many other influencers throughout our nation that contributed significantly as well. But, the abject violence during the miners' struggle stands out as the most extreme example for labor reform. Also, the miners faced life or death working conditions, which made it even more pressing during this era. It was the Wild West of the East. Appalachia had yet to be tamed.

I also give credit to Thomas Felts, and to a lesser degree his brothers Albert and Lee. If Ed Chambers and Sid Hatfield had not been murdered by Baldwin Felts detectives, there likely would not have been the Blair Mountain disaster. But because this major event happened, it would have been relatively fresh in the minds of Congress in 1938. All the other labor conflicts would be as well. That said, nothing moves rapidly in Congress unless their poll numbers are tanking. Historically, laws take time to be created, or at least they used to. The miners of West Virginia probably didn't know this. Whether or not, in Matewan, they waited over 50 years for our Federal government to remedy the most Draconian working conditions in American history, excluding slavery.

At the junction of Route 52 and Highway 65, the Wirt Marcum Memorial Bridge crosses over Pidgeon Creek. This is the primary road to get to Matewan.

Remembering Wirt

It is tempting to continue writing about the foundation and evolution of American unions, which I find fascinating. But this work is not really about that subject. Because Sid Hatfield fought so hard for basic working rights through the early unionization efforts, it's interesting to explore their past, which is his past. Where the unions go in the future is hard to say. This work is not intended to either promote or injure the institutions that collectively bargain for a working contract. I believe a free market economy can support both union and non-union workers.

The relationship between the employer and employee around the turn of the 20th century was mostly governed by the imperfect laws that were written. I don't really agree with the Lochner Act, but it was the law of the land. Much has changed since 1920. I provide these facts to better understand the dynamic of a Representative Republic style government. It's not perfect. But, it's not possible to create a government that is politically perfect and satisfies all of its subordinates. Human nature simply does not allow this. There will always be the disenfranchised and the malcontents who clamor for a different way. They've been around since Moses.

There is no difference with making laws in America. There has never been a poll that found all citizens 100% compliant with any issue or debate and there never will be. Americans blend the circumstances of the times with the needs of the moment to decide our future. But, we're not perfect and we never will be. Dred Scott and Korematsu are the first examples that come to mind, but there are many more. We learn from our mistakes and we are free to correct those mistakes. That's what separates us from any other government, nation or culture, in the history of mankind. We are free to admit our errors and we are free to correct those errors. That freedom is not an option in

Cuba, or Venezuela today. It was not an option in the former Soviet Union and it's certainly not an option in China. The difference between America and most every other society in history is that we can evolve from our past. The people can vote, and it still matters. We are not without sin, but we have the freedom to correct those sins.

The purpose of this work is to celebrate the life of Sid Hatfield and his legacy of influencing basic worker rights in America. The fact that he was highly associated with Blair Mountain connects him (in my opinion) to the political events that followed over the next two decades. Blair Mountain was a big deal to the masterminds of Washington DC. It certainly got their attention. They knew this event was significant and they knew it could happen again. Some, maybe most, realized the void of fairness in the written laws of the time. They probably saw the tragic death of Sid Hatfield as one of many examples to change things. They would have remembered this 20-year-old event. Just like America had many Founding Fathers, so too did the creators of the American working rights we enjoy today. I believe Sid was one of them.

The other big idea is that Sid was a great influencer of the need for workplace safety and child labor regulations. He was a common victim of child labor exploitation in the pre-war coalfields of West Virginia. There were thousands of young people who were abused, harassed and underpaid just like him. He was an unusual dude, but he had the smarts to realize something was wrong. He also had the guts to do something about it. He was a fighter who refused to stay down after he was beaten. This work is intended to demonstrate the impact a highly motivated individual can have on society. Agree or disagree with Sid, at least he did "something."

The last part of this work is dedicated to a remote GPS in Mingo County, WV. The community is called Red Jacket. To be honest, there's not much there. However, in the early 1980's when I was a traveling salesman for a spice company, I had a small account there known as Wirt's Market. The store sat on the banks of Pigeon Creek. The owner was a grumpy and disagreeable old man named Wirt Marcum. He has long since passed away. At the time, he owned a small grocery store at the junction of Hwy 52 (King Coal Highway) and WV Route 65. Route 65 will take you over the mountain to Matewan. (Remember the 10% grade picture earlier?) Anyway, this old store was inundated with coal dust. Coal trucks would fly past this store at dangerous speeds. 80+ MPH were common. These trucks were open top 18 wheelers, by and large, and they were driven by people who just wanted to get home after a hard day of work. Their conversations on the CB radio were colorful, to say the least. These were the days before talk radio. The Citizens Band radio was all the rage. These drivers were like the earliest foundation of Twitter today, albeit, a much smaller audience. They had no filters, and none were expected. If you had to drive two plus hours to get home from a long day at work, their conversations split that time in half. It almost made you look forward to an otherwise miserable experience.

Particles of their payload would swirl into the store and settle on everything inside. The store was only yards away from Route 65 and Hwy 52. The single cash register was made out of 2 X 4's and particleboard--screwed together with drywall screws, I assume. The floors looked like they were last cleaned during the Spanish-American War. In the entire box, there were only three aisles and they were so narrow that only one customer could shop at a time. Wirt's office (a small space near the front door) was where he stored the cigarettes and chewing tobacco. (High theft items). He would sit in a crusty old rocking chair that looked like it came over on the Mayflower. He gave the impression he was oblivious to anything happening. But he saw everything. He was the emperor of this tiny kingdom. This much was not in doubt.

Wirt never bought a single case from me. But he was on my call list because of the distributor I represented. As a manufacturer's representative, I was required to service all the businesses the distributor supplied--big or small. I faithfully paid a visit to this cranky old man every other week. I would go inside, introduce myself and whip out my real ostrich feather duster. I knocked off the coal dust from the products I represented, and even some of the products I didn't represent. (I'm just a nice guy.) I faced up my sections, ever watching for a glimpse of Wirt's main assistant. On my way out, I always made sure to make a purchase. At minimum, it was a grape NeHi soda from his open top cooler by the front entrance. It was a "returnable" bottle that needed a bottle opener. The bottle opener was a wall mounted unit located on the frame of the front door. It had been painted over at least 20 times throughout the years, but it worked just fine. I would throw a dollar on the register, pop the top, and wave goodbye as Wirt would grunt at me while he devoured his Styrofoam container of food.

Before I made my final departure from Wirt's world, I always peered around one last time hoping to get a glimpse of Wirt's "right hand man." I will never know her name, but she was the most beautiful woman I had ever seen. She had long brown hair and she always wore tight Levi's and a loose sweatshirt. Wirt would send her over the Pigeon Creek bridge to the only drive in restaurant in town. She would walk back with a Styrofoam container of lunch, and/or breakfast, in a brown paper bag. She faithfully walked over that bridge, bought the food, and promptly brought it back to Wirt, probably for years. He would sit in that rocking chair and eat. No one bothered him while he ate. No, no, no. As far as I remember, she only spoke to me once or twice over the many years.

I had only two motivating factors that kept me calling on this account. One, my company required it. Two, I wanted to catch a glimpse of the most beautiful woman in the world, or so I believed. Each time I left this account it was exactly the same as the time before. Wirt sat in that chair and I couldn't bring myself to present any new items, promotions or discounts. That was supposed to be my job, but what was the point? This was Wirt's world. And so it was.

Throughout all the years I worked in this territory, I don't think I ever saw Wirt get out of his rocking chair. My final picture is all that's left of this era. When I stopped to take a picture of this memory, there were three or four local citizens sitting on the steps of a small-town grill across the creek from Wirt's original store. This would have been where the old drive-in restaurant was. Wirt's old grocery store is where a very nice convenience store currently sits today. Just like Wirt, they have most everything you need. And they're very nice people.

The locals were all smoking a cigarette and checking their cell phones. As I moved about the property, one of them eventually shouted out to me. "Hey, what are you doing here?" I was startled right away. Afterall, I'm walking around someone's property. I explained that I was trying to find an old memory. "There was an old grocery store here," I said. As soon as I spoke those words, they were suddenly pleasant and helpful. When I described the old man sitting in the rocking chair, they immediately knew who I was talking about. "That was Wirt Marcum!" one of them shouted. "He's dead."

We talked for a few moments and I soon realized there was absolutely nothing left of this memory. I thanked them for their assistance and loaded up for the next part of my journey. I had many hundreds of miles in front of me. But at least, it was warm with rain showers off and on throughout the day. The parking lot was cloaked in mud and sparsely scattered gravel. Great pools of muddy water lay waiting to further soil my beleaguered sedan. At least that part of my memory had not changed. I felt a strange sense of satisfaction. I just visited a place that will never be the same as it was when I worked there years ago. Nor will it be the same as it was 100 years ago. This is when you realize . . . Ok, move on. It can only be a memory now. I hope Sid found the peace to enjoy one of these moments in his life. He certainly earned it. Like so many times in our Earthly journey, you just sigh and then you smile. And you say, "it was good enough."

Realizing the hard miles ahead, it was time to go.

⤸ The End ⤹

Acknowledgements

I would also like to recognize my father, Harry "Buddy" Beckett, from Barboursville, WV. His accomplishments in this life are numerous. Aside from being a great father, he has written six books. He provided his family with security, faith, and a real chance of happiness.

Kudos to Greg Jones, a great friend, and Rick Webb, a great cousin. Their feedback had a major influence on this book. I would also like to recognize Kathi Sherrill. She is the Matewan Public Library director. Her contribution to my effort was instrumental. Without her support, this work would not be.

And finally, I would love to acknowledge a lifelong citizen of Matewan who helped me in ways I cannot fully express. I promised I would not include names or identities, and I did not. This is the most difficult part of this work. What this person did for me can never be fully understood. I can only say thank you. I sincerely hope you enjoy this book. You, more than anyone else, created it. God bless you.

CPSIA information can be obtained
at www.ICGtesting.com
Printed in the USA
BVHW091942300421
606221BV00013B/1711